HISTORICAL ANTHOLOGY OF MUSIC

ORIENTAL, MEDIEVAL, AND RENAISSANCE MUSIC

Historical Anthology
OF
MUSIC

BY
ARCHIBALD T. DAVISON AND WILLI APEL

ORIENTAL, MEDIEVAL AND RENAISSANCE MUSIC

REVISED EDITION

39813

HARVARD UNIVERSITY PRESS
CAMBRIDGE, MASSACHUSETTS

LIBRARY OF CONGRESS CATALOG CARD NUMBER 49-4539

ISBN 0-674-39300-7

Printed in the United States of America

PREFACE

THE query is sometimes raised as to why, in view of their acknowledged value, there are not more anthologies of music; and why there is not at least one which may be said to be truly representative in scope, or one which puts before the reader a reproduction of the material free from those compromises which seem to be an inevitable feature of such compilations. Best qualified to answer this question are those who have attacked the problem actively and who know from experience that the flawless anthology of music belongs to that imaginary world in which lifetimes are at least twice as long as those we now enjoy, where knowledge is boundless, where financial caution is unknown, where human error is non-existent, and where publication is the plaything of idealists. Proceeding under such limitations as at present exist, the editors of a work of this kind must, to the best of their ability, attempt to realize two objectives: first, the compilation of a body of music which, by itself and without regard to any practical usefulness, represents a comprehensive survey of the music of any given period; and second, the selection, where choice is possible, of material which will prove profitable to the most varied types of musical interest. The editors have striven to attain these two objectives, and—again with due regard for inescapable limitations— they hope that in the main they have succeeded. If their ambitions have been realized, this volume should prove useful alike to the musicologist, the amateur, the practical musician, the student, and the teacher; and as it illustrates the styles, idioms, and technical procedures typical of the periods represented, it should find ready place as a textbook in courses in music history such as are offered in colleges and conservatories.

There is here a considerable amount of music which the editors believe has not heretofore appeared in modern notation. Much, but by no means all of this, is drawn from the medieval period; and some of it, certainly, has not been previously transcribed. A goodly portion of this "new" material is to be found in the music of the twelfth to the fourteenth centuries, a period of the greatest significance, especially to advanced students of music history. In view of Dr. Apel's experience in the medieval field it was agreed that he should assume final responsibility for the music in that section, and the above-mentioned transcriptions are entirely his work. These illustrations, like others which will be generally unfamiliar, were not chosen for their novelty. They were included because they seemed most representative.

In the highly controversial matter of editorial accidentals the editors have adopted the practice, now coming more and more into general acceptance among scholars, of employing the utmost reserve. Those who feel that reticence in this detail has been overemphasized may, of course, deal with the question of the accidentals as they see fit.

Foreign texts are translated, many of them quite literally. Such virtue as might be claimed for the paraphrase has, in general, been consciously forsworn through the conviction that in a work of this nature the exact meaning of each foreign word is more valuable than a statement of the approximate meaning of a whole passage. Thus, taken by themselves, some of the translations may at a first reading appear baffling; but when referred to the original their sense, we hope, will become clear. There is a brief commentary for each number, with reference to the source of the selection.

Reference will be found to phonograph records of a number of the selections. In order to supply these the editors had recourse to the usual sources of information; but being aware of the rapidly changing catalogues of the various phonograph companies, they make no pretense to thoroughness in this department of the work. Furthermore, they have not even heard a measurable proportion of the records cited and they therefore wish to disclaim any responsibility for the value of this feature. If the records are found to be useful, that will certainly justify their mention.

The editors have been in agreement from the outset as to the principles which should govern the selection of the examples. Each piece must be a complete composition or a whole movement from a larger work, as for instance, the Agnus Dei from a Mass or the Secunda Pars of a motet. Each selection must illustrate something historically or technically important. And underlying the whole procedure of choice has been the conviction that no music should be offered, regardless of its historical or technical fitness, which could not lay claim to consideration on grounds of artistic significance. Such slight departures from these principles as have been made represent no more than compromises inevitable in a volume subject to the normal limitations of space.

The first compromise—an obvious one—and so necessary as to be a compromise in name only, concerned the reduction of scores to practical, readable size. Vocal scores of six or eight staves, orchestral pages of ten or twelve, may present no difficulties to the expert musician; but for the average student they would render a volume such as this relatively useless. The prime requirement is, of course, that all the notes of any selection shall appear; and after that, that the music shall be available for as many grades of reading ability as possible. But reduction unquestionably raises a difficulty; for it sometimes yields a bewildering array of stems which are necessary for keeping clear the progress of several voices written on the same staff. Only where the persistent use of the correct stemming would have produced a quite unreadable result, notably in certain passages of No. 157, have the editors been willing to compromise with necessity. The editors feel that, under almost any conditions, difficulties due to stemming are not comparable with those imposed in the reading of a full score. Furthermore, to have issued the selected material in open score would have confined a comparatively small segment of music history to a single volume and would have swollen the whole work to a library of encyclopedic proportions.

In the vocal pieces it has seemed the part of wisdom to avoid repeating the text whenever coincidence of the notes with the syllables to which they belong is self-evident. And this has seemed a particularly desirable compromise in the case of reduced scores, where to have included every word would have needlessly cluttered up a page already not innocent of complication. In spite of conscientious effort, no uniform system for indicating word-omission has proved practicable, but we believe that such devices as the brace to indicate the use of the same text by two adjacent voices and successive dots to signify text-repetition will be found sufficiently clear. In all cases the editors have employed abbreviation of the text only where, they believe, ambiguity is impossible.

A compromise which dictated the use of expert copying instead of the customary printing process is one which may bring some objection. Printing is doubtless more satisfactory, but it is also more expensive; and in the opinion of the editors its superiority is not sufficiently marked to offset an advantage to the purchaser which permits the sale of the volume at a relatively low figure.

All compromises with the exception of the last-mentioned have been of an entirely practical nature; that is, they represent an effort to avoid visual complication and thus facilitate the reading of the score. In attempting to achieve this end, however, the editors have occasionally found themselves unable to employ an entirely consistent method of notation. Where three voices occupy a single staff, for instance, the voices absent from any one measure will be accounted for by separate rests; where all the voices are silent, it has been thought that one rest would prove an adequate substitute for three.

As the work progressed the editors have become convinced that adherence to the principles upon which the project was founded would necessitate the distribution of the material through two volumes rather than one, as originally planned: the first volume to include Oriental, Medieval, and Renaissance music; the second, now in preparation, to continue to approximately 1800. Even so, division of the work into two volumes, while it has solved one major editorial problem, has in no sense destroyed the persistent dilemma of what to choose and what to omit from an initial list of very measurable proportions. The question has never been one of finding enough illustrative material, but rather of deciding what, regretfully, must be left out. As a practical reinforcement to the Anthology the authors have in mind the writing of a history of music and the issuing of records, both based upon the contents of this volume and the one to follow.

A grant from the William F. Milton Fund of Harvard University has aided the editors substantially in assembling the material; and for this they are deeply grateful. Another financial contribution, no less gratefully received, has been made by the Carl Schurz Memorial Foundation, Philadelphia. Hearty recognition is offered for the generous assistance of those who have contributed much of value to this volume. Among them are several to whom we are indebted for music which is the fruit of their own research. Following is a list of these, together with the numbers they supplied us: Dr. Armen Carapetyan, No. 113; Professor Edward Lawton, No. 161; Professor Oliver Strunk, No. 66; Professor Alfred Einstein, No. 158; Mr. Elmer Olsson, Nos. 67 and 71; Mr. Alfred Zighera, No. 176. Advice regarding the selection of certain numbers has been gratefully received from Professor Alfred Einstein, Dr. Manfred F. Bukofzer, Mr. Gordon Sutherland, and Mr. Siebolt Frieswyk.

The bulk of the translating was done by Mr. Benjamin Bart, Teaching Fellow in Romance Languages in Harvard University. Other translations were generously supplied by the following, all of Harvard University: Professor Yuen Ren Chao, No. 2; Professor Walter E. Clark, No. 4; Professor Harry A. Wolfson, No. 8;

Professor Werner Jaeger, No. 7; Professor William C. Greene, No. 6; Professor Taylor Starck, Nos. 20, 24, 60, 81, 87, 93; and Professor George B. Weston, Nos. 47, 49, 54, 91, 95, 96, 123, 130, 131, and 160. For the translation of No. 22a we are indebted to Miss Caroline B. Bourland of Boston; and to Miss Isabel Pope of Cambridge for translations of Nos. 22b, 22c, 97, and 98.

Too much cannot be said for the skill and devotion of Mr. Alfonso Pasquale of New York, on whom fell the responsibility of making all the final copies, with the exception of five which are the work of Mr. John Scabia of Boston.

During the years which have been occupied with the preparation of this volume the editors have been constantly aware that all their ambitions could not be fulfilled. Especially have they feared that considering the number of hands through which the manuscript must pass in the course of its preparation the hope of bringing out a volume in which every note and every word should be presented with undeviating accuracy is not likely to be realized. They will not be surprised, but they will be grateful, if readers will inform them of errors.

Whatever opinion may be held of the validity of the contents from the standpoint of inclusiveness, or of educational or artistic value, it may be said sincerely that the editors have tried conscientiously to balance the many factors involved, and to select and reject accordingly. Endeavoring to avoid what appeared to them to be the shortcomings of previous anthologies, they have, at the same time, added what they believe to be some features of positive value. Nor have they accepted the necessary compromises without trying to wring from them what virtue they could. Their ablest apologist is, of course, the music itself. For that no excuses need be made.

Cambridge, Massachusetts
December 1945

For the editors,
A. T. D.

PREFACE TO THE REVISED EDITION

The musical material contained in the first issue of Volume 1 of the Historical Anthology of Music here remains intact with one exception: No. 76, mistakenly ascribed to Obrecht, has been withdrawn and in its place have been substituted Nos. 76a and 76b. We are grateful to Father Alex. J. Denomy, C.S.B., for the translation of No. 76a.

In the preface to the first volume the editors forecast that fair percentage of errors which is an almost inevitable feature of the initial printing of a music collection. At the same time, the editors humbly besought users of the book to notify them of any mistakes which might be discovered. The response to that request has been most generous, and the editors wish to express their thanks to the following who have been especially helpful: Margaret Dewey, Western College, Oxford, Ohio; Charles Warren Fox and his seminar at the Eastman School of Music, Rochester, New York; Charles Goodman, Grace Church Rectory, Yantic, Connecticut; A. Tillman Merritt, Harvard University, Cambridge, Massachusetts; Daniel Pinkham, Boston; Robert Tangeman, Juilliard School of Music, New York City.

This revision represents a much closer approach to accuracy than did the first edition, and the editors sincerely hope that readers will apprise them of any further changes which should be made in subsequent printings.

Cambridge, Massachusetts
September 1948

For the editors,
A. T. D.

CONTENTS

CHAPTER I

ORIENTAL AND GREEK MUSIC

CHAPTER II

EARLY MEDIEVAL MUSIC
——— (400–1300) ———

CHAPTER III

LATE MEDIEVAL MUSIC
——— (1300–1400) ———

CHAPTER IV

EARLY FIFTEENTH CENTURY

CHAPTER V

LATE FIFTEENTH CENTURY

CHAPTER VI

EARLY SIXTEENTH CENTURY

CHAPTER VII

LATE SIXTEENTH CENTURY

COMMENTARY AND TRANSLATIONS

ORIENTAL, MEDIEVAL, AND RENAISSANCE MUSIC

I. Ancient and Oriental Music

1. Chinese

a. Entrance Hymn for the Emperor

c. 1000 B.C.

b. Instrumental piece for flute and guitar

Modern

2. Japanese

Fuki No Kyoku

Accompanied song

Fu- ki to   yu   mo   ku- sa no   na

3. Siamese

Kham Hom (Sweet Words)   Orchestral piece

4. Hindu

Sâman: two versions

1. From the ancient notation.
2. From a phonographic recording.

1.

three times

hā-u hā-u hā-u āj-ya-do-ham[-ma] mūr-dhā-nan-dā-i vā- a-ra-tim pṛ-thiv-yā[-ḥ] vaiś-vā-na-rām[-a] ṛ-ta ā

2.

M ♩ = 73½

jā-ta-ma-gnim[-a] ka-vi-[m-]sam-rā jā ma-ti thiñ ja-nā-nām[-a] ā- san-naḥ pā-trā-an ja-na- yan-ta de-vā[-ḥ]

twice

hā-u hā-u hā-u āj-ya-do-ham[-ma] āj-ya-do- hā-u vā e āj-ya-do-ham[-ma] e āj-ya-do-ha-hā- m ham-mā

5. Arabian

Popular song

Scale   Introductory model. Free tempo

elwárdu jinḥa-leẑ î-dâríẑẑ innadâ haddek walrusnu jindabel

jâ 'idâ hebbunasîme qád- dek waẑẑimsu tiẑbahe za-mâ- lek wamâlqámer

'ábedek wa enta jâ sájjadî ilmilâh lâ qáblek wa lâ ba-dek

Two Singers. ♩ = 114

6(3/4)

jâ wibena-wî ta nâ-ri 'a-lâ zer- zî- se wib-na- wî ta-jā nâ-ri 'al-

Drum jâ wibena-wî ta-ja zâ-wissa-baj-ja zâ-u-wissa-

Skin Frame

6(3/4)

Bagpipe

Fine.

1.   2.

lâ zer- zî- se web-na wî-ta-jā äs-'ar-hā twî- la 'a-lis- dir-

baj-ja 'a-lū zā- wî-ta t'amile ta-wî- le ū tzíb-hā-

7

Da capo with new text

6. Jewish

a. Accents (Ta'amim), Syrian

b. Syrian intonation of the Pentateuch

c. Ledovid boruh (Psalm 144): four versions

7. Greek

a. First Delphic Hymn

c. 138 B.C.

A

Ke-klyth' He- li-ko- na ba-thy- den-dron hai la-che-te Di-os e- ri- bro-mou-ou thy-ga-tres eu- o- le-noi.

Mo-le-te syn-o- mai-mon hi-na Phoi-oi-bon o- da-ei- sin mel-pse-te chry- se-o-ko-man, Hos a-na di-ko-

ryn-ba Par- nas- si- dos ta-as-de pe-te- ras he-dran ham'a- ga- kly-tai-eis De-el-phi-si-in Ka-sta-li-dos

e-ou-y- drou na-mat' e-pi- nis-se- tai, Del- phon a-na pro-o- na ma-an-tei- ei-on e-phe-pon pa- gon.

B

En kly-ta me-ga-lo-po- lis At-this eu-chai-ei- si phe-ro- ploi-o nai- ou-sa Tri- to-o-ni-dos da-pe-don a-

thrau-ston, Ha-gi- ois de bo- moi-oi-sin Ha-phai-stos ai-ei- thei ne-on me-ra-ta-ou- ron, Ho-mou-ou

de nin A-raps a-tmos es O- lym-pon a-na- kid-na-tai. Li- gy de lo- to-os bre-mon a-ei-o- loi-ois

me-les-in o- da-an kre-kei. Chry-se- a d'a- dy-throus ki-tha-ris hym- noi-sin a- na- mel-pe- tai.

b. Hymn to the Sun

Mesomedes of Crete (c. A.D. 130)

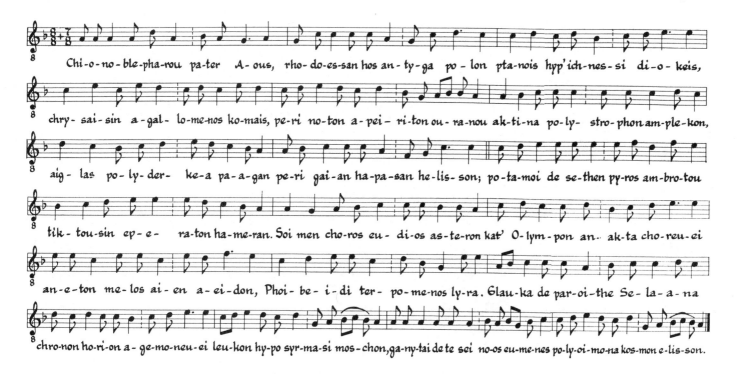

Chi-o-no-ble-pha-rou pa-ter A- ous, rho-do-es-san hos an- ty-ga po- lon pta-nois hyp'ich-nes-si di-o-keis,

chry- sai-sin a-gal- lo-me-nos ko-mais, pe-ri no-ton a-pei- ri-ton ou-ra-nou ak-ti-na po-ly- stro-phon am-ple-kon,

aig- las po-ly-der- ke-a pa-a-gan pe-ri gai-an ha-pa-san he-lis-son; po-ta-moi de se-then py-ros am-bro-tou

tik- tou-sin ep-e- ra-ton ha-me-ran. Soi men cho-ros eu- di-os as-te-ron kat' O-lym-pon an- ak-ta cho-reu-ei

an-e-ton me-los ai- en a- ei-don, Phoi- be- i-di ter- po-me-nos ly-ra. Glau-ka de par-oi-the Se- la-a- na

chro-non ho-ri-on a- ge-mo-neu-ei leu-kon hy-po syr-ma-si mos-chon, ga-ny-tai de te sei no-os eu-me-nes po-ly-oi-mo-na kos-mon e-lis-son.

Ho-son zes phai-nou, me-den ho-lo-os sy ly-pou-ou. Pros o-li-gon e-es-ti to ze-en, to te-los ho chro-nos a-pai-tei-ei.

8. Byzantine Chant (13th Century)

a. Ode for Christmas

E-so-se la-on thau-ma-tur-gon des-po-tes hy-gron tha-las-ses ky-ma cher-so-sas pa-lai, he-kon de tech-theis

ek ko-res tri-bon ba-ten po-lon ti-the-sin he-min; hon kat' ou-si-an i-son te pa-tri kai

bro-tois do-xa-zo-men.

b. Hymn from the Octoechos

Hym-nou-men ton so-te-ra, ton ek tes par-the-nou sar-ko-then-ta, di' he-mas gar e-stau-ro-the kai te tri-

ta he-me-ra an-es-te, do-rou-me-nos he-min to me-ga e-le-os.

II. Early Medieval Music (400-1300)

A. Liturgical Monophony

9. Ambrosian Hymns

a. Aeterne rerum conditor: three melodies

Ae-ter-ne re-rum con-ditor, Noctem di-em-que qui re-gis, Et tempo-rum das tem-po-ra, Ut al-le-ves fa-sti-di-um.

b. Aeterna Christi munera: two versions

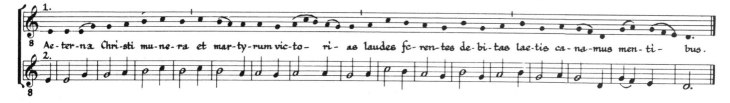

Ae-ter-na Chri-sti mu-ne-ra et mar-ty-rum vic-to- ri- as laudes fe-ren-tes de-bi-tas lae-tis ca-na-mus men-ti- bus.

10. Ambrosian Chant

Verse "Eructavit" of the Gradual "Speciosus Forma"

1. In Ambrosian (Milanese) chant.
2. In Gregorian (Roman) chant.

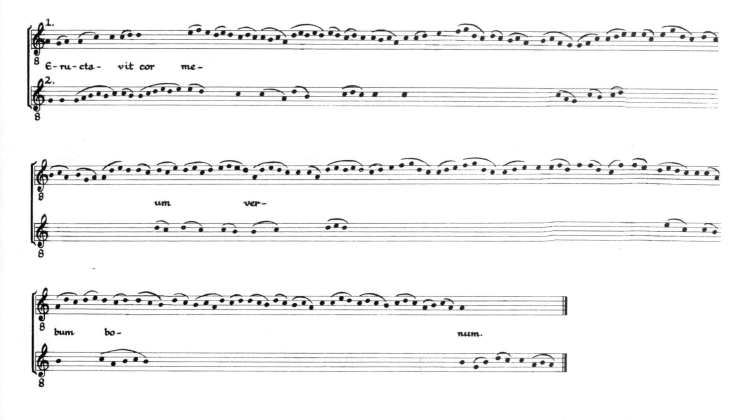

E-ru-cta- vit cor me-

um ver-

bum bo- num.

11. Gregorian Chant

Psalm 146 with antiphon

Lauda-bo. 1. Lau-da anima mea Do-mi-num, laudabo Dominum in vi-ta me- a: psallam Domino meo quam-di- u fu-e-ro.
2. Noli confidere in prin-ci-pi-bus: in filiis hominum in qui-bus non est sa- lus.
9. Dominus custodit ad-ve-nas, pupillam et/ viduam sus-ci-pi-et: et vias pecca ——— to-rum dis-per- det.
D. Gloria pa ——————————————tri et fi-li-o: et spi ——— ri-tu-i san- cto,
Sicut erat in principio et nunc et sem- per: et in saecula sae ——— cu-lo-rum. A- men.

Antiphon.

Lau-da-bo De-um me-um in vi-ta me-a.

12. Gregorian Chant

Gradual: Haec dies

13. Gregorian Chant

Alleluia: Angelus Domini

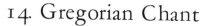

14. Gregorian Chant

Responsorium: Libera me

15. Gregorian Chant

a. Kyrie IV: Cunctipotens

Ky-ri-e   e-   le-i-son.(3times) Chri-ste   e-   le-i-son (3)

Ky-ri-e   e-   le-i-son (2) Ky-ri-e   e-   le-i-son.

b. Kyrie-Trope: Omnipotens

Tuotilo (d. *c.* 915)

1. Om-ni-po-tens ge-ni-tor, De-us om-ni-um cre-a-tor: e-   ley-son. 1.Chri-ste, De-i for-ma vir-tus
2. Fons et o-ri-go bo-ni, pi-e lux-que per-en-nis: e-   ley-son. 2.Chri-ste, patris splen-dor, or-bis
3. Sal-vi-fi-cet pi-e-tas tu-a nos, bo-ne rec-tor:e-   ley-son. 3.Ne tu-a dam-ne-mur Je-su

pa-tris-que so-phi-a: e-   ley-son. 1.Am-bo-rum sa-crum spi-ra-men ne-xus a-mor-que: e-   ley-son.
la-psi re-pa-ra-tor: e-   ley-son. 2.Pro-ce-dens fo-mes vi-tae, fons pu-ri-fi-cans nos: e-   ley-son.
fac-tu-ra be-nig-ne: e-   ley-son.

3. Pur-ga-tor cul-pae, ve-ni-ae lar-gi-tor op-ti-me, of-fen-sas de-le, sanc-to nos mu-ne-re re-ple: e-   ley-son.

16. Sequences

a. Alleluia: Dominus in Sina, with Sequence: Christus hunc diem

Notker Balbulus (d. 912)

Al- le- lu- ia   ℣Do- minus in Si-na in san-   cto, as-cen-dens (etc.)

1.Christus hunc di-em jo-cundum cun-ctis con-ce-dat es-se Chri-sti-a-nis a-ma-to-ri-bus su-is. 2.Chri-ste Je-su, fi-li De-i,
3.Of-fi-ci-is te An-ge-li

me-di-a-tor na-tu-rae no-strae ac di-vi-nae, Ter-ras, De-us, vi-si-ta-sti ae-ter-nus, ae-the-ra no-vus ho-mo trans-vo-lans.
at-que nu-bes sti-pant ad pa-trem re-ver-su-rum. Sed que mi-rum, cum lac-tan-ti ad-huc stel-la ti-bi ser-vi-ret et An-ge-li ?

4. Tu ho-di-e ter-re-stri-bus rem no-vam et dul-cem de-di-sti, do-mi-ne, spe-ran-di coe-le-sti-a. 6. Quan-ta gau-di-a tu-os re-
5.   Te ho-mi-nem non fic-tum le-van-do su-per si-de-re-as me-tas regum, do-mi-ne. 7. Quis de-di-sti cer-ne-re, te

plent a-po-sto-los, 8. Quam hi-la-res in coe-lis ti-bi se-cur-runt no-vi or-di-nes 10.Quem, Christe, bo-ne pastor, dignare custodire.
coe-los per-ge-re. 9. In hu-me-ris portanti di-u dis-per-sum a lu-pis gre-gem u-num.

b. Victimae paschali laudes

Wipo (*c.* 1000–1050)

Vi-cti-mae pa-scha-li lau-des im-mo-lent Chri-sti-a-ni. A-gnus re-de-mit o-ves: Christus in-no-cens Pa-tri re-con-ci-li-a-vit
Mors et vi-ta du-el-lo con-fli-xe-re mi-ran-do dux vi-tae mortu-us

pec-ca-to-res. Dic no-bis Ma-ri-a, quid vi-di-sti in vi-a? Se-pul-crum Chri-sti vi-ven-tis, et glo-ri-am vi-di resurgentis.
re-gnat vi-vus. An-ge-li-cos te-stes, su-da-ri-um, et ve-stes. Sur-re-xit Chri-stus spes me-a: prae-ce-det su-os in Ga-li-le-am.

Sci-mus Chri-stum sur-re-xi-sse a mor-tu-is ve-re: tu no-bis, vi-ctor Rex, mi-se-re-re. A-men. Al-le-lu-ia.

c. Jubilemus Salvatori

Adam de St. Victor (12th century)

I
Ju-bi-le-mus Sal-va-to-ri quem ce-le-stes laudant cho-ri con-cor-di le-ti-ci-a.
Pax de ce-lo nun-ci-a-tur, ter-ra ce-lo fe-de-ra-tur, an-ge-lis ec-cle-si-a.

II
Ver-bum car-ni co-u-ni-tum, sic-ut e-rat
Vir-go pa-rit, De-i tem-plum, nec ex-em-plar

III
pre-fi-ni-tum, si-ne car-nis co-pu-la, Res est no-va, res in-si-gnis quod in ru-bo ru-bet i-gnis, nec ru-bum at-ta-minat.
nec ex-em-plum per tot ha-bens se-cu-la. Ce-li ro-rant, nu-bes plu-unt, mon-tes stil-lant, col-les flu-unt, ra-dix Jes-se germinat.

IV
De ra-di-ce flos as-cen-dit quem pro-phe-te pre-os-ten-dit e-vi-dens o-ra-cu-lum; Mi-ra flo-ris pulchri-tu-do quem commendat
Ra-dix Je-sse re-gem Da-vid, vir-ga ma-trem pre-si-gna-vit vir-gi-nem, flos par-vu-lum. Re-cre-e-mur in hoc flo-re qui nos gu-stu,

V
ple-ni-tu-do sep-ti-for-mis gra-ti-e; Jhe-su, pu-er im-mor-ta-lis, tu-us no-bis hic na-ta-lis pa-cem det et gau-di-a;
nos o-do-re, nos in-vi-tat spe-ci-e. Flos et fru-ctus vir-gi-na-lis cu-ius o-dor est vi-ta-lis, ti-bi laus et glo-ri-a.

VI

B. Religious and Secular Monophony

17. Latin Lyrics (Conductus)

a. Song of the Ass

1. O-ri-en-tis par-ti-bus Ad-ven-ta-vit a-si-nus Pulcher et for-tissi-mus Sar-ci-nis ap-tis-si-mus, Hez, Sir As-ne, hez.
4. Aurum de A-ra-bi-a, Thus et myrrham de Sa-ba Tu-lit in ec-cle-si-a Virtus a-si-na-ri-a, Hez, Sir As-ne, hez.
7. A-men di cas, a-si-ne, Iam sa tur de gramine, A-men, a-men i-te-ra, As-per-na-re ve-te-ra, Hez, Sir As-ne, hez.

b. Christo psallat (Rondellus)

1. Chri-sto psallat ec-cle-si-a, 3. Re-dempta Si-on fi-li-a 4. Det lau-dem re-gi glo-ri-ae,
2. Mi-tis mi-se-ri-cor-di-a, 5. Mi-tis mi-se-ri-cor-di-a; 6. Mor-tem de-stru-xit ho-di-e.

c. Beata viscera

Perotinus (c. 1160 — c. 1220)

Be-a-ta vi-sce-ra Ma-ri-e vir-gi-nis, Ve-ste sub al-te-ra vim ce-lans nu-mi-nis, Dic-ta-vit fe-de-
cu-jus ad u-be-ra rex ma-gni no-mi-nis,

ra De-i et ho-mi-nis. O mi-ra no-vi-tas et no-vum gau-di-um, Ma-

tris in-te-gri-tas post pu-er-pe-ri-um.

d. Sol oritur

Sol o-ri-tur in sy- de- re Ro- ri com-par in vel- le- re Et lu- ci-fer in

ve- spe-re Se- re-nat um- bra lit-te-rae. In- ta-cto sem-per

la- te- re Vir-gi-nis et pu- er-pe-rae Pro-dit pro-

les de- i- ca.

18. Troubadours

a. Pax in nomine (Vers)
Marcabru (d. *c.* 1150)

1. Pax in ro-mi-ne Do-mi-ni! Fetz Mar-ca-brus los motz e'l so. Au- jatz que dit: Cum nos a fait, per sa dous-sor, Lo
5. Probet de li-gnat-ge Ca- ï Del pri-meiran ho-me fel-ho, A tans ais-si C'us a Dieu no por-ta ho- nor. Vei-

Scingno- rius ce- le- sti- aus Pro-bet de nos un la-va-dor C'anc fors ou-tra-mar n'on fon taus En de lai de-ves
rem'qu'ill er a- mics co- raus C'ab la ver-tut del la- va-dor Nos se- ra Jhe-sus co- mu- naus, E tornem los gar-

Jo- sa- phas, E d'a- quest de sai vos co- nort.
ssos a- tras Qu'en a- gur cre-zon et en sort.

b. Be m'an perdut (Canzo)
Bernart de Ventadorn (d. 1195)

Be m'an per-dut lay en- ves Ven-ta-dorn Tuih mei a- mic pos ma do-na no m'a- ma.
Non ay ra- zon que ieu ia mays lai torn Tant es vas mi bra-va e nos re- cla-ma.

Tot iorn me fai sem-blan i- rat e morn Car en s'a-mor mi de- lieg em so- jorn E de res als nos ran-

cu- ra nis cla- ma.

c. Reis glorios (Canzo): three rhythmic interpretations
Guiraut de Bornelh (d. *c.* 1220)

1. (Anglés)

Qu'en

2. (Gérold)

3. (Besseler)

1. Reis glo-ri-os, ve- rai lums e clar-tatz 3. Al meu com-panh si- as fi- zels a- iu- da,
2. Deus po-de-ros, sen- her, si a vos platz,

1.
2.
3. Qu'eu non la vi pos la noitz fon ven-gu- da, Et ad-es se-ra l'al- ba.

d. Kalenda maya (Estampie)

Raimbault de Vaqueiras (d. 1207)

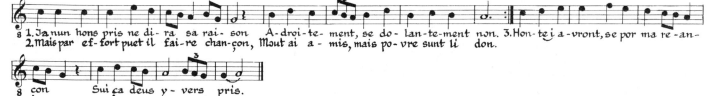

1. Ka- len- da ma- ya Ni fuelhs de fa- ya Ni chanz d'au-zelh Ni flors de gla- ya 3. Del vo-stre belh Cors
2. Non es que'm pla- ya, Pros dom-na gua- ya, Tro qu'un y-snelh Mes-sa-tgier a- ya 4. Pla- zer no-velh Qu'a-

qu'em re-tra- ya

mors m'a- tra- ya, 5. E ja- ya E'm tra- ya Na vos dom-na ve-ra- ya. que'm n'e-stra- ya.
6. E cha- ya De pla- ya'L ge-los ans

19. Trouvères

a. Ja nuns hons pris (Ballade)

Richard Coeur-de-Lion (1157–1199)

1. Ja nun hons pris ne di- ra sa rai- son A-droi-te- ment, se do- lan-te-ment non. 3. Hon-te i a-vront, se por ma re-an-
2. Mais par ef-fort puet il fai-re chan-çon, Mout ai a- mis, mais po-vre sunt li don.

çon Sui ça deus y- vers pris.

b. Quant voi (Ballade)

Perrin d'Agincourt

1. Quant voi en la fin d'es- tey La fuil- le che- oir 3. Lors ai de chan-ter vo- loir Grei- gnour
2. Et la grant jo- li- ve- tey D'oi- seaux re- me- noir

que je ne se- loi- e Car ce- le a cui je m'ou-troi- e Li- ge- ment, M'en a fait com-man-de-ment, Si

chan-te- rai: Et quant ma-da- me plai- ra Joie a- vrai.

c. Douce dame (Ballade)

1. "Dou- ce da- me de- bon- nai-re." "Fau-vel que te faut?" 3. "Ne vous en chaut il?" "Fi, mau- vais ou- til."
2. Mon cuer vous doins sanz re- trai-re." "Sen en toi de- faut."

"Puis qu'en- si est que fe- rai?" "Ja m'a- mours ne te le- rai."

d. En ma dame (Rondeau)

I.

1. En ma dame ai mis mon cuer 2. Et mon pen-ser. 3. N'en par-ti-roi a nul fuer, 4. En ma dame ai mis mon cuer, 5. Si m'ont sor-pris si vair

6. oeil 6. vi-ant et cler: 7. En ma dame ai mis mon cuer 8. Et mon pen-ser.

II. A

1.4.7. En ma dame ai mis mon cuer 2.8. Et mon pen-ser

3. N'en par-ti- roi a nul fuer 6. Vi-ant et cler.

5. Si m'ont sor- pris si vair oeil

e. Vos n'aler (Rondeau)

Guillaume d'Amiens

1.4.7. Vos n'a-ler mi-e si com je faz 2.8. Ne vos, ne vos n'i sa-vez a-ler, Ne vos, ne vos n'i sa-vez a-ler.

3. Bele A-a-liz par main se le-va 6. Bonjor ait ce- le que n'os no-mez So-vant m'i fait e- le sou-pi-rer.

5. Biau se ves-ti et mieuz se pa-ra

f. C'est la fin (Virelai)

I. A

1. C'est la fin, koi que nus di- e, j'a-me-rais. 2. C'est la jus en mis les prés, 3. C'est la fins, je veul a-

mer, 4. Jus et baus i a le-ves, bele a- mie ai. 5. C'est la fin koi que nus di- e, j'a- me-rais.

I. a

1.5. C'est la fin, koi que nus di- e, j'a- me-rais. 2. C'est la jus en mis les prés,

4. Jus et baus i a le-ves, bele a- mie ai. 3. C'est la fins, je veul a- mer,

g. E, dame jolie (Virelai)

1.5. E, da-me jo-li- e, Mon cuer sans fau-ceir Met en vos-tre bai-li- e Ke ne sai vo peir.

4. Si for-ment m'a-gri- e Li douls malz d'a-meir Ke par sa si-gno-ri- e Me co-vient chan-teir:

2. So- vant me voix con- plai-gnant Et an mon cuer do- lo-sant D'u- ne ma-lai-di- e

3. Dont tous li mous an a- mant Doit a- voir le cuer jo-iant Cui teilz malz mais-tri- e.

h. Pour mon cuer (Rotrouenge)

1. Pour mon cuer re- le- e-cier Vueil u- ne chan-çon fe- re, 4. Cer-tes ja de li a- mer ne

2. Chan-ter vous vueil sanz ten-cier D'u- ne mult de- bon-nai- re, 5. Se li cous de-voit a- voir brui-

3. Que j'ai-me de cuer en- tier Or dont dex qu'il i pai- re.

se- rai las Car ele a tres-tout mon cuer pris en sez laz.

siez les bras Si a-vrai je de sa fa- me mes de graz.

i. Espris d'ire (Lai)

Guillaume le Vinier

1. Es-pris d'ire et d'a- mour, Plaing ma hau-te fo- lour, Dont j'ai joie et pa- our Plus de mil fois cascun jour. Teus est ma vi- e:

2. Joie ai de ma tris-tour Et duel de ma bau- dour. Bien pert de mon mil- lour Quant pour joie et pour dou-cour De mort m'a-fi- e.

17

20. Minnesingers

a. Swa eyn vriund

Spervogel (12th century)

Swa eyn vriund dem andern vriunde bi-ge-stat Mit gantzen truwen gar an alle missetat, Da ist des vriundes helfe gût. Dem er sie willichliche tut, Daz sie geli-che einander helen, Dem meret sich daz kunne.

Swa vriunde eynander wege sint, Daz ist ein mi-chel wunne.

b. Nu al 'erst (Bar)

Walther von der Vogelweide (d. 1230)

1. Nu al-erst lebe ich mir wer-de Sit min sün-dic ou-ge siht
2. Hie daz land und auch die er-de Den man vil der e-ren giht.
3. Mirst ge-schehen des ich je bat:

Ich bin kom-men an die stat Da got men-nisch-li-chen trat.

c. Der May

Neithart von Reuenthal (d. c. 1240)

Der may hat me-nig her-cze hoch er-stai-gett Sprach ein maid, er hatt es wohl er-czai-get. Was sein su-sser wun-ne thut,

Wann er klai-det swar-czen dorn in wei-sse plût. Al-les das der wint-ter hett be-czwun-gen Das wil der may nu jun-gen.

1. Win-der wie ist nu dein kraft Wor-den gar un-si-ge-haft Seyt der may- e sei- nen schafft Auff dir hatt zu-sto-chen.
2. Vor den wäl-den auff der plan Sieht man vol-kumen-li-chen stan Liech-te plümb-lein wol-ge-tan Der han ich ge-pro-chen.

3. Gar be-sun-der durch ein wunder sol-ches kun-der ich ver-nahm, Man und fraw-en ir sult schawen in den aw-en o- ne scham,

Wie des lich-ten may-en schar Stet be-clait in pur-pur far. Jun-gen maidt das neh-met war, blei- bet un-ver-spro-chen.

21. Laude (13th Century)

a. Gloria in cielo

Glo- ri-a in cie-lo e pa-ce in ter-ra Nat' è'l no-stro sal'-va-to-re. Nat'è Cri-sto glo-ri- o- so

L'al-to Dio ma- ra-vi-glio- so Fa-cto è om de- si- de- ro-so Lo be-ni-gno cre- a-to-re.

b. A tutta gente (Ballata)

1.5. A tut-ta gen- te fa- cio pre-gho e di- co Che lau-di me-co Mar-ga-ri-ta au- len-te.
4. An-ci pren-de- ste la fe- de cri-sti-a- na Che sca-cia va-na et fa a Dio ser- ven-te.

2. O ver-gi- ne, che'n pic-co-la e- ta- de A Di- o vi de-ste e fo-ce- vi sua spo-sa
3. Et non vo-le-ste per no-bi-li-ta- de Che foss' en vo-i es- ser del mon-do ro-sa.

c. Santo Lorenzo (Ballata, modified)

1.5. San-to Lo- ren- zo mar-tyr d'a- mo-re, A Cri-sto fo- sti gran- de ser-vi-do- re.

2. Con hu- mil- ta-de Al san- cto pa- dre Fo-sti u- bi-di-en-te
3. Per cio lau- da-re Sem- pre de fa- re Tut-ta l'u- ma-na gen-te

4. Per te, mar- tir va-len-te et di va- lo-re; Al 'ni-po- ten- te se' au-len-te flo- re.

22. Cantigas (13th Century)

a. A Madre (Villancico)

R. A Ma-dre do que liu-rou Dos le-õ-es Da-ni- el, Es-sa do fo-go guardou Un me-nyn-no d'Is-ra-el.

I. En Be-or-ges un ju-deu Ou-ve, que fa-zer sa-bi- a Vi-dro, et un fil-lo seu Que el en mais non a-vi- a
XI. Por e-ste mi-agr'a- tal Log'a ju-de-a cri-ý- a, Et o me-nyn-no sen ál O ba-tis-mo re-ce-bi- a;

Per quant end'a-prendí eu Ontr'os cris-chã-os li-ý- a Na es-col', e e-ra greu A seu pa-dre Sa-mü-el.
Et 'o pa-dre que o mal Fe ze-ra per sa fo-li- a Dé-ron ll'enton mor-te qual Quis dar a seu fill' A-bel.

b. Mais nos faz (Villancico)

1.5. Mais nos faz san-cta Ma- ri-a A seu fil- lo per-dõ- ar Que nos per no-ssa fo- li- a Ll'i mos fa- lir et er-rar.
4. En o y-ffer-no en-tro-u Mais a do mui bon ta-lan Tant'a seu fillo ro-go-u Que o foy end' el sa-car.

2. Por e- la nos per- dõ- ou Deus lo pe-ca- do d'A-dam,
3. Da man-çã-a que go-stou Por que soff-reu muit af-fan.

c. Aque serven (Villancico)

1.5. A- que ser-ven to-do'-los ce- le-sti- a- es Gua- re-cer ben po- de as cha-gas mor-ta- les
4. Gran fi-an-ça en e- la, et a ser-uí- a Põ-en-do ant' o seu al-tar e-sta-da- es.

2. D'est' un gran mi- ra-gre fez San- ta Ma-ri- a
3. De Sa-las por hũ a mol-ler que a-uí- a

23. English Songs

a. Sainte Marie

St. Godric (d. 1170)

I.
Sainte Ma-ri-e virgi-ne, Moder Jesu Cristes Na-za-re-ne, On-fo schild help thin God-ric, Onfong bring

II.
he-gi- lich with the in Go-des ri-che. Sain-te Mari- e Cri-stes bur, Maidenes clen-had, moderes flur;

Di-li-e min sin-ne, rix in min mod, bring me to win- ne with the selfd God.

Worl-des blis ne last no throw-e Hit wit and wend a- wey a- non. The len-gur that hich hit i know-e, The lasse hic

fin-de pris ther on. For all hit is i-meynd wyd ka-re. Mid sor-rew-e ant wid u-uel fa- re. Ant at the las-te pou-re

ant ba-re, Hit let mon wen hit gin-net a- gon. Al the blis-se this he-re ant the-re, bi-lonketh at hen-de wop ant mon.

24. Mastersingers

Der Gülden Ton (Bar)

Hans Sachs (1494–1576)

1.Lob sei Gott Va- ter in dem Thron, schon, fron, der uns sein Wort, der Gna- den Hort,
2.dar- durch wir clar den wil- len sein, fein, rein, er- ken- nen hy, on zwei-ffel y,

an man-nig Ort, yez gne-digk-lich auss- rifft. 3.Die vor was gar ver-dun-kelt sehr von der sched-li-
clar lau-ter wy auss der hei- li- gen Schrifft.

chen Men-schen Lehr, die uns pracht in der Zwei-ffel schwer; der her ver- hen-get uns

das, seit uns viel bass liebet die strass mensch-li - cher lug und gifft.

C. Early Polyphony (to 1200)

25. Parallel Organum

a.

Scholia enchiriadis (c. 850)

1. Organum of the octave

Nos qui vivimus benedicimus Dominum ex hoc nunc et usque in saeculum.

2. Organum of the fifth
Vox principalis

Composite

Vox organalis

3. Organum of the fourth
Vox principalis

Composite

Vox organalis

b. *Musica enchiriadis* (c. 850)

1.
Pr.
Or.
Sit glo-ri-a Do-mi-ni, in sae-cu-la lae-ta-bi-tur Do-mi-nus in o-pe-ri-bus su-is.

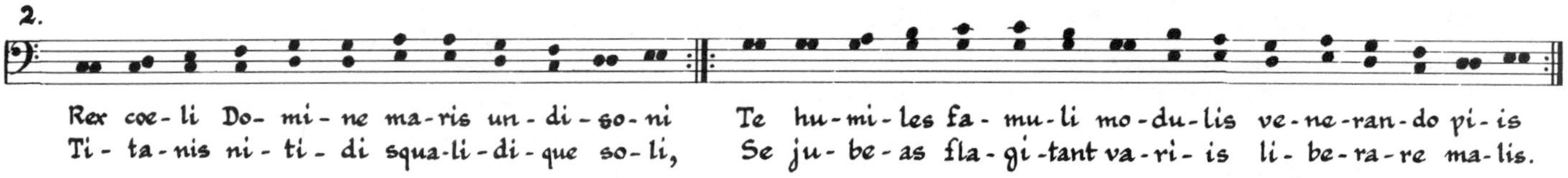

2.
Rex coe-li Do-mi-ne ma-ris un-di-so-ni Te hu-mi-les fa-mu-li mo-du-lis ve-ne-ran-do pi-is
Ti-ta-nis ni-ti-di squa-li-di-que so-li, Se ju-be-as fla-gi-tant va-ri-is li-be-ra-re ma-lis.

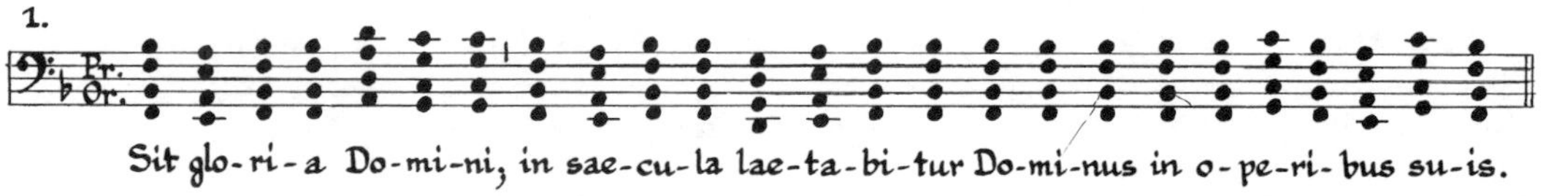

c. Hymn to St. Magnus 12th century

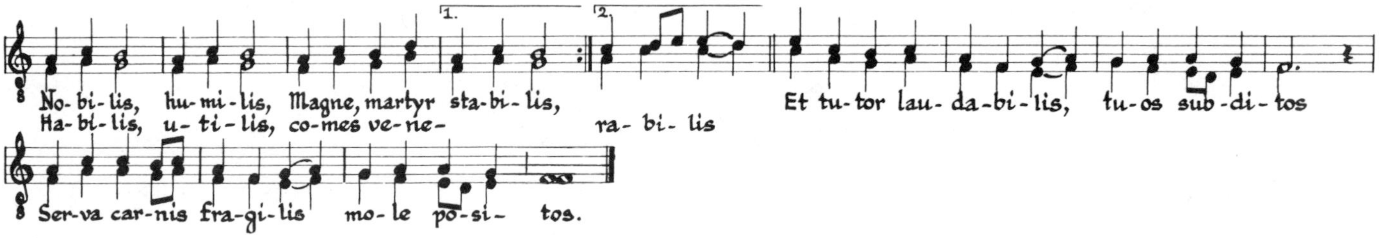

1.
2.
No-bi-lis, hu-mi-lis, Magne, martyr sta-bi-lis, Et tu-tor lau-da-bi-lis, tu-os sub-di-tos
Ha-bi-lis, u-ti-lis, co-mes ve-ne- ra-bi-lis
Ser-va car-nis fra-gi-lis mo-le po-si- tos.

26. Free Organum

a. Cunctipotens genitor 11th century

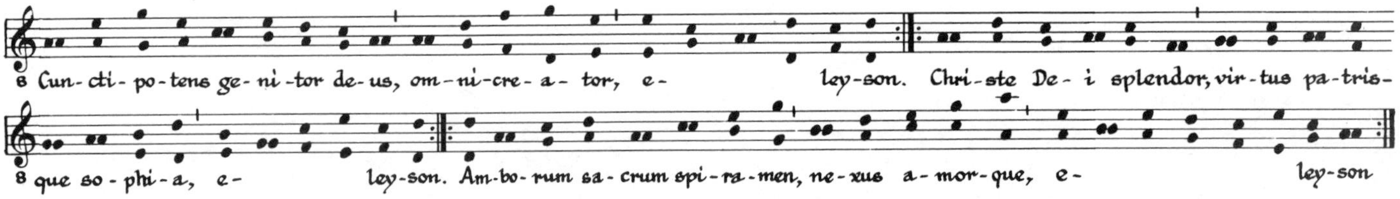

Cun-cti-po-tens ge-ni-tor de-us, om-ni-cre-a-tor, e- ley-son. Chri-ste De-i splendor, vir-tus pa-tris-
que so-phi-a, e- ley-son. Am-bo-rum sa-crum spi-ra-men, ne-xus a-mor-que, e- ley-son

b. Ut tuo propitiatus 11th century

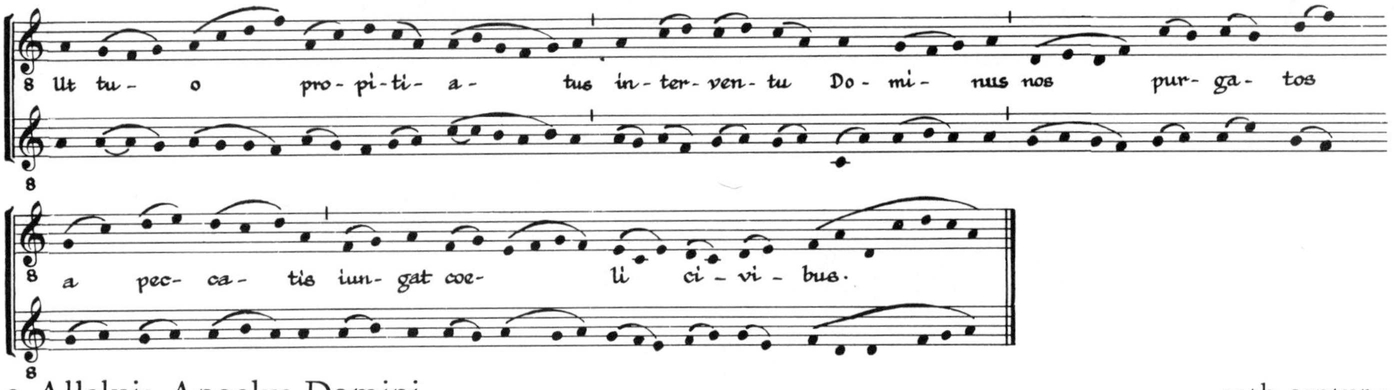

Ut tu- o pro-pi-ti- a- tus in-ter-ven-tu Do-mi- nus nos pur-ga- tos
a pec- ca- tis iun-gat coe- li ci-vi-bus.

c. Alleluia Angelus Domini 11th century

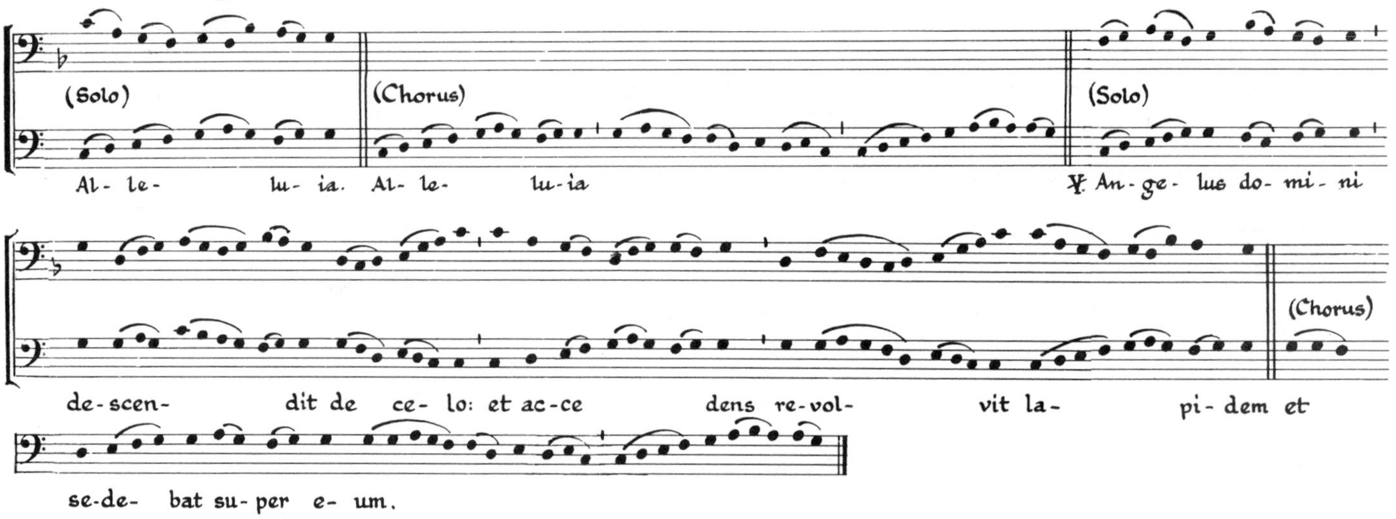

(Solo)
(Chorus)
(Solo)
Al-le- lu-ia. Al-le- lu-ia ℣. An-ge-lus do-mi-ni
(Chorus)
de-scen- dit de ce-lo: et ac-ce dens re-vol- vit la- pi-dem et
se-de- bat su-per e- um.

27. Melismatic Organum

a. Viderunt Hemanuel

School of St. Martial (c. 1125)

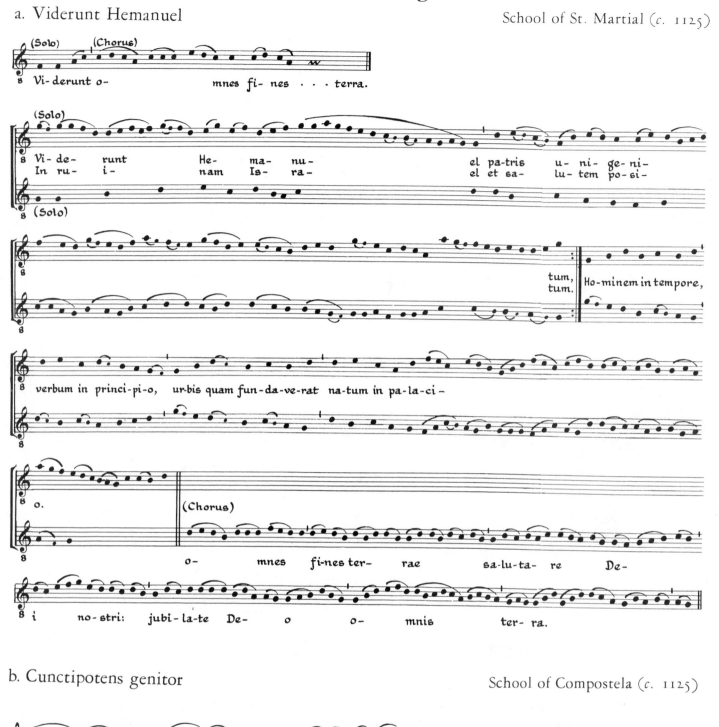

Vi-derunt o- mnes fi- nes . . . terra.

Vi-de- runt He- ma- nu- el pa-tris u- ni- ge- ni-
In ru- i- nam Is- ra- el et sa- lu- tem po-si-

tum, Ho-minem in tempore,
tum.

verbum in princi-pi-o, ur-bis quam fun-da-ve-rat na-tum in pa-la-ci-

o.

(Chorus)

o- mnes fi-nes ter- rae sa-lu-ta- re De-

i no-stri: jubi-la-te De- o o- mnis ter- ra.

b. Cunctipotens genitor

School of Compostela (c. 1125)

Cun- cti- po- tens ge- ni- tor, De- us om- ni- cre- a-

tor, e- ley- son. Cri- ste, De- i

for- ma, vir- tus pa- tris-que so- phi- a, e- ley- son.

Am- bo- rum sa- crum spira-men ne-xus a-mor- que, e- ley- son.

23

28. Benedicamus Domino:
Plainsong, Organa, Clausulae, Motets

a. Plainsong

Be- ne- di-ca-mus Do-
℟. De——— o gra-
mi- no.
ti- as.

b. Two-voice organum

School of Compostela (*c.* 1125)

Be- ne- di- ca- mus Do-
mi-
no.

c. Two-voice organum

School of Notre Dame (*c.* 1175)

Be———
ne———
di———
ca———
mus———
Do———
mi——— no.———

d. Domino (Clausula)

School of Notre Dame (*c.* 1200)

(Chorus)   (Soloists)

Be- ne- di-ca-mus DO-
MI-

NO. (Chorus) De- o gra- ti - as.

e. Domino (Clausula) School of Notre Dame (*c.* 1200)

DO-

[MI- NO. DO-]

MI- NO

f. Domino fidelium — Domino (Motet) School of Notre Dame (*c.* 1225)

Do- mi-no fi- de- li- um Om-ni- um fi- de-lis de- vo- ci- o Lau-dis cum pre-co-ni- o Ju- bi- let in

Do ————

gau- di- o Cu- ius be- ne-fi- ci- o Vi- ta re-sti- tu- i- tur. Re-di-me- at ab ex- i- li- o

Ple- bis na- ti- o Post cul- pe re-me-di- um Sub-it pa- tri- e pa-tris pre- di- um.

mi ——— no.———

g. Dominator — Ecce — Domino (Motet) School of Notre Dame (*c.* 1225)

Do- mi-na-tor Do- mi-ne Qui de vir-gi- ne Ma-tre na-tus im-mo-la- tus Es pro ho- mi-ne, Mun- da

Ec- ce mi-ni-ste- ri- um Pro-fert al-vus vir-gi-nis Mi- re lu- cis ra-di-um Pri-mi tol-lit ho- mi-

Do ————

25

nos a cri-mi-ne Ut le-ti plau-su ge-mi-no Ti-bi si-ne ter-mi-no Be-ne- di-ca-mus Do- mi- no.

nis Par-tus i-ste vi-ci-um Nunc si-ne fi-na-li ter-mi-no Hym-num re-fe-ra-mus Do- mi- no.

mi - no.

h. Clausula and derivative motet

School of Notre Dame

1. Clausula: Domino

(c. 1200)

Do-

mi - no.

2. Motet: Pucelete — Je languis — Domino

(c. 1250)

Pu-ce-le-te bele et a-ve-nant Jo-li-e-te, po-lie et plei-sant, La sa-de-te que je de-sir tant Mi fait liés,

Je lan- guis des maus d'a- mours. Mieuz aim as-sez qu'il m'o- ci- e Que nul

DOMINO

[Do——

jo-lis, en-voi-siés et a- mant. N'est en mai ein-si gai rous-signolet chan-tant S'a-me-rai de cuer en-tie-re-ment M'a-mi-e-te

au- tre maus. Trop est jo- li- e la mort. A-le- giés moi,

la bru-ne-te jo-li-e-te-ment. Bele a-mi-e qui ma vie en vo baillie a-ves tenu-e tant; Je vos cri mer-ci en sou-pi- rant.

douce a- mi- e Ces- te ma-la-di- e Qu'a-mours ne m'o-ci- e.

mi — no]

i. Tenor: "Flos Filius," with Clausula (I), Latin motet (II),
and French motet (III)

School of Notre Dame (c. 1250)

29. Organum

Hec dies

In Leoninus style (c. 1175)

di ———

es

[Chorus]

quam fe-cit   Do- mi - nus: exsul- te-   mus

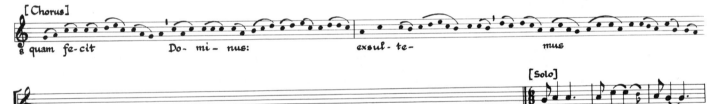

[Solo]

[Solo]

et lae-te- mur in e- a. ———   ℣. Con ——   fi —

te ——   mi ——

[Clausula]

ni Do ——   mi ——   no

28

[Chorus]

8 mi- se- ri- cor- di-a e- jus.

D. Thirteenth-Century Polyphony

30. Clausulae for "Hec Dies"

[Solo]

8 Hec   di —

8   es   quam fe-

8 cit   Do- mi- nus: exsul- te-   mus   et lae- te-

8 mur in e-   a   V. Confi- te- mini Do-

8 mi -   no

8   Quo-

8   ni -   am   bo-   nus, quo- ni- am

[Solo]

8 In   se-   cu- lum

[Chorus]

mise- ri- cor- di-a e- jus.

30

31. Organum

Hec dies

Hec

di-

[Chorus]

es   quam fe- cit ... e-a.   ℣.Con-   fi-   te-   mi-

ni   Do——   mi-   no

quo-

ni-

am bo-

nus

32. Motets for "Hec Dies"

a. Huic main — Hec dies

Huic main au doz mois de mai De- souz le so- lau le- vant, En un ver- gier m'en en- trai.

HEC DIES

De- sous un pin ver- doi- ant U- ne pu- cele i tro- vai Ro- ses coil- lant. Lors me trais vers li De

fine a- mour la pri. E- le me res pon- dit: A moi n'a- tou- che- res vos ja Qar j'ai mi- gnot a- mi.

32

b. O mitissima (Quant voi) — Virgo — Hec dies

c. Deo confitemini — Domino

d. Trop sovent — Brunete — In seculum

Trop so- vent me dueil   Et sui en grie- té   Et tout por ce- li   Qui j'ai tant a- mé

Bru- nete a   qui j'ai mon cuer do- né   Por voz ai maint grief mal en- du- ré.   Por Deu! pre- gne

IN SECULUM

[In se ———]   cu- lum]

Par son grant or- gueil   Et par sa fier- té.   A ma dame ai mis   mon cuer   et   mon pen- sé.

vos de moi pi- té   Fins cuers a- mo- rous!   De de- bo- nai- re- té vient   a- mors.

e. Instrumental motet: In seculum

IN SECULUM

33. Two Motets

a. Alle, psallite — Alleluya

b. On parole — A Paris — Frèse nouvele

sent, Car il n'est si bon-ne vi- e Que d'estre a ai- se   De bon cler vin et de cha- pons, Et d'estre a-

ne char et   bon pois-   son, De tou- tes guises compai-gnons,   Sens sou- ti-

se nou-   ve-   le!   Muere fran- ce, muere, muere fran-   ce!   Fre-

veuc bons com- paignons, Liés et joi- ans, Chantans, truf-fans et a-mo-rous,   Et d'a- voir, quant c'on

e, grant bau-   dour, Biaus joi-aus da- mes d'ou-   nour, Et si truev' on bien

se nou-   ve-   le!   Mue-re fran- ce, muere, muere fran-   ce!   Fre-   se nou-

a mes-tier, Pour so- la- cier Be-les da-mes a de-vis: Et tout ce truev'on a Pa- ris.

en-   tre-deus De menre   feur pour ho-mes de-   si-   teus.

ve-   le!   Muere fran-   ce,   muere, muere fran-   ce!]

34. Motet

Aucun— Lonc tans —Annuntiantes

Petrus de Cruce (d. c. 1300)

Aucun ont trouvé chant par u-sa-ge, Mes a moi en doune ochoi- son   Amours, qui resbaudist mon coura-ge Si que m'es-tuet faire   chan-

Lonc   tans   me   sui te-nu de   chan-   ter,

ANNUN[TIANTES]

çon.   Car a-mer me fait da-me bele et sage Et de bon re-non;   Et je, qui li ai fait houmage, Pour li servir tout mon

Mes or ai rai-   son de joi-   e   me- ner,   Car   bou-

36

35. Motet

Je cuidoie — Se j'ai — Solem

Period of Petrus de Cruce

Je cuidoi-e bien metre jus Le dous mestier d'amour, Mais je me sentoi-e plus Que devant sou-pris-douce-ment D'une amour nouve-

Se j'ai fo- le- ment a-

SOLEM

le. De la gra-ci-eu-se te Qui a a non dou-cete A son droit non. Ele est si tres douce voire-ment Que je cuide bien certainement

mé, Et moi mout gre- vé Sans a- le-

Que Dieus et nature i a-pe-le-rent amour A fourmer si faite cre-a-tu-re; Car en li ne faut riens qu'e-le ne soit

ge- ment, Ce set mon cuer qui le sent;

a mourouse-te par fai-te-ment. Ele est brunete, sa-de-te, Cointe, jonette, Grailete, saverousete, Et plus que nul autre jo-li-e-

Cie- re- ment l'ai com- pa-

te; A la boucete En dous ris vermeillete, Plaisan-ment; Simplete en sa manierete Est, et de bel con-te-ne-ment;

re. Mais or sui bien a mon gré D'a- mours as-

38

Son dous cler vi-ai-re monstre qu'ele est debo-naire: Ce me fait en grant joie esperer de li merci prochaine-ment.

se- né, Qui tous biens rent, Et

Si l'aim si bien, Dous Dieus! que j'i pring Bel o-coi-son de dire: Se j'ai a-mé trop folement autre que li, je m'en repent. S'en gra-

pour ce, d'amer si tres fo-le- ment,

ci de cuer bone a-mour Que apres dolour, Par ma folour, Grant douchour me rent.

je m'en re- pent.

36. Adam de la Halle (*c.* 1230-1287)

a. Li maus d'amer   Monophonic ballade

1.Li maus d'a- mer me plaist miex a sen- tir K'a mainta- mant ne fait li dons de joi- e,
2.Car mes es- poires vaut d'au-trui le jo- ir. Si bien me plaint quan-ques a-mours m'en- voi- e.

3.Car quant plus suff-re et plus me plaist que soi-e Jo-lis et chan- tans. Aus- si

liés sui et joi- ans Que se plus a- vant es-toi- e.

b. Tant con je vivrai   Rondeau

1.4.7.Tant con je vi-vrai 2.8.N'a- me- rai au- trui que vous.
3.   Jà n'en par-ti-rai 6. Loi-au- ment mis m'i sui tous.
5.   Ains vous ser-vi-rai

39

c. Diex soit

1.3.5. Diex soit en ches- te mai- son Et biens et joie à fui- son. 2. No si- res no- veus Nous en-
4. No si- res est teus Qu'il pri-

voie a ses a- mis; Ch'est as a- mou- reus Et as courtois bien a- pris, Pour a- voir des
e- roit à en- vis; Mais as frans hon- teus Nous a en son lieu tra- mis, Qui som- mes de

pa- rei- sis A no- he- li- son.
ses nou- ris Et si en- fan- çon.

37. Two-Voice Trope

Rex virginum   Early 13th century

1. Rex, vir- gi- num a- ma- tor, De- us, Ma- ri- ae de- cus, e- ley- son.
2. Qui de stir- pe re- gi- a pro- du- cis Ma- ri- am, e- ley- son.
3. Pre- ces e- ius sus- ci- pe di- gnas pro mun- do fu- sas, e- ley- son.

1. Christe De- us de pa- tre, ho- mo na- tus Ma- ri- a ma- tre, e- ley- son.
2. Quem ven- tro be- a- to Ma- ri- a e- di- dit mun- do, e- ley- son.
3. Su- me lau- des no- stras, Ma- ri- ae al- mae di- ca- tas, e- ley- son.

1. O pa- ra- clite ob- umbrans cor- pus Ma- ri- ae, e- ley- son. 3. Qui su- per celos spi- ritum le- vas Ma-
2. Qui di- gnum facis tha- lamum pec- tus Ma- ri- ae, e- ley- son.

ri- ae, Fac nos post ipsam scandere tu- a vir- tu- te, Spi- ri- tus al- me e- ley- son.

40

38. Two-Voice Conductus

Roma gaudens jubila

Early 13th century

Ro- ma gau-dens ju-bi-la, Men-tis pro-cul nu-bi-la Splen-
dor ex-pel-lat ho-di-e Splendor pa-cis et glo-ri-e Fi-de-li-bus lu-gen-ti-bus Or-
tus de tu-o prin-ci-pe. Sy-on er-go fi-li-a Sur-
ge de tri-sti-ti-a! Sa-lu-tis ad-est do-mi-nus, Ut tu-o
fi-at ter-mi-nus Ex-i-li-o cum gau-di-o; Jam re-gem re-gum
sus-ci-pe.

39. Three-Voice Conductus

Hac in anni janua

Early 13th century

Hac in an-ni ja-nu-a, hoc in ja-nu-a-ri-o tenda-mus ad ar-du-a vir-tu-tum sub-

41

si- di- o. Gau-di- a sunt mu-tu- a, mu-to fac-to vi-ti- o; re-pro-bo- rum

fa-tu- a re-pro-ba-tur a- cti- o

E. Thirteenth-Century Dances

40. Monophonic Dances

a. Danse Royale   Ductia

b. Danse Royale   Estampie

c. English Dance

Estampie

41. Two-Voice Dances

a. Ductia

b. Ductia

III. Late Medieval Music (1300-1400)

42. Sumer Is Icumen In (c. 1310)

43. Roman de Fauvel

Isorhythmic motet

Huius modi quid dampnabilius. Jugier se doit reison et non li-eus De pingue qui o vice-domi-ne Par te-le gent prin-
ont Men- da- ci- is tam-quam nu-gi-ge-ri Plus c'on ques

ce ont determiné In su- bi-tos quos-cunque gras-sa-ri Dont est pi-tié s'en sont plusieurs ma- ri Ecclesi-as palam expo-li-
mès a gens sont en-the-ri. Hi de-fe-ce bi-bunt et fa-ci-unt Duques a donc que bienfait ont pe-

ant Sur es-pe-ce de bien mal pa-li-ant Juste de-us de-tracto-res su- e De leur me-dis car ils sont trop li- ne.
ri Hos duc, de-us ad por-tas in-fe- ri.

44. Guillaume de Machaut (1300-1377)

S'il estoit nulz   Isorhythmic motet

S'il e- stoit nulz qui pleindre se de-ust pour nul mes- chief que d'amour re- ce-
S'a- mours tous a- mans jo-ir au com-man-ce-

ET GAUDEBIT COR VESTRUM

ust; je me devroi-e bien pleindre sans re-traire; car quant pre-miers me vint enamou-
ment fai-soit, son pris fe- roit a- men-rir,

46

rer, on-ques en moy har-dement de-mou-rer ne vost lais-si-er de ma dolour re-trai-re;

car nuiz a- mans ne sa- roit les grans

mais ce qui plus me faisoit res-jo- ir et qui e- spoir me donnoit de jo- ir en

de- duis c'on re- coit en da- me d'on- nour ser- vir.

res-gardant, sans plus di- re ne fai-re, fist de- par- tir de moy; puis en pri-son

Mais cil qui vit en de- sir, et bonne

el- le me mist ou j'euc ma li-vri-son de ardans desirs qui si me tient con-trai- re

A- mour l'a- per- coit, en a plus qu'il

que, se un tout seul plus que droit en e- usse, je scay de voir que vi-vre ne pe-us-se sanz le secours ma- dame de

ne vou- droit, quant joi- e li wet me- rir. Et pour

bon- nai- re   qui m'a de ci, sans morir res-pi-té. Et   c'est bien drois car doucour en pi-

ce   nulz re- pen- tir   de bien

té   et cour-toi-si- e ont en li leur re-pai-   re.

a- mer ne se   doit, s'A-mours le fait trop lan-guir.

45. Guillaume de Machaut

Je puis trop bien

Ballade

Ct.
Je Dy-   puis trop bien ma   da-me com-pa-rer a l'y- ma- ge
voi- re fu, tant belle et si sans per que plus l'a- ma

T.

|1   que fist Pyma-li- on.
|2   que Me-de-e Ja-zon. Li   folz toudis la pri- oit, mais l'y-ma-ge riens

ne li respon-doit. Eins-si me fait cel- le   qui mon cuer font, qu'a-   des la pri et rien ne me re-spont

46. Guillaume de Machaut

a. Comment qu'a moy

Virelai

1.5. Com-ment qu'a moy lon-tein-ne soi-es, da-me d'on-nour, si m'e-stes vous pro-chein-ne par pen-ser nuit et jour.
4. vo ma-nie-re cer-tein-ne et vo fre-sche cou-lour qui n'est pa-le ne vein-ne, voy tou-dis sans se-jour.

2. Car Sou-ve-nir me mein-ne, si qu'a-des sans se-jour
3. vo biau-te sou-ve-rein-ne, vo gra-ci-eus a-tour,

b. Plus dure

Virelai

1.5. Plus du-re que un dy-a-mant ne que pier-re d'a-y-mant est vo dur-té, da-me qui n'a-
4. par un ac-cueil at-trai-ant, m'ont au cuer en re-sgar-dant si fort na-vré que ja mais joi-

ves pi-té, de vostre a-mant qu'o-ci es en de-si-rant vostre a-mi-tié.
e na-vré, ju-sques a-tant que vo gra-ce qu'il a-tant m'au-res don-né.

8.2. Da-me, vo pu-re biau-té qui tou-tes passe, a mon gré, et vo sam-blant
3. simple et plein d'u-mi-li-té, de dou-ceur fi-ne pa- ré, en sous-ri-ant,

47. Jacopin Selesses (Late 14th Century)

En attendant

Ballade

En a- ten-ten- dant es-pe-ran-ce con-for-te
en a- ten- dant se de-duit et de-por-te

Contratenor

l'hou- me qui vuet a-
en a-ten- dant un

Tenor

orig:

49

voir per- fec- tion
pre- mier guer- re-
(re)-

don.
En a- ten- dant

pas- se temps et sai- sum en at- ten- dant met

en li sa fi- an- ce de tous ce mes est ser-

vi a fui- son Cilz qui ne set viv- re sans

es-pe- ran-

ce.

48. Baude Cordier (fl. *c.* 1400)

a. Amans ames

Rondeau

1.4.7.A-
3. Re-
5. Car

mans
ce-
qui-

a-
ues
con-

mes
cest
ques

se-
en-
fait

cre- te-
sai- gne-
aul- tre-

[ment]

ment 2.8. Si
ment 6. D'a-
ment

lon-
mour

gue-
il

ment
fait

vo-
le

les
doulx

a-
a-

mer.
mer.

b. Belle bonne

Rondeau

1.4.7.Bel-le bon-ne sa-
3. De re-ce-voir ce
5. Car tant vous aim

ge plai-san- te
don ne soy- es
qu'ailleurs n'ay mon

et gen-
len-
en- ten-

Contratenor

Tenor

te,   A ce jour cy que l'an se re-nou-   vel-
te,   Je vous sup- pli, ma dou-ce de- moi-   sel-
te,   Et sy scay que vous es-tes seu- le   cel-

le 2.8.Vous fais le don d'u- ne chan- so nou-vel-   le   De-dens mon
le 6. Qui fame a-ves que chas-cun s ap-pel-   le: Flour de beau-
te

coeur qui a vous se pre-sen-te.
te sur toutes ex- cel-len-te.

49. Jacopo da Bologna (fl. *c.* 1350)

Non al suo amante   Madrigal

1. Non   al so a-man-te piu Di- a- na pia-mi la pas- tu-re-la al-pe-stra e cru-
2. C'a   mi la pas- tu-re-la al-pe-stra e cru-

1. Non   al so a-man- te   piu Di- a- na pia-
2. C'a   mi la pas- tu-   re-la al-pe-stra e cru-

que   Quan-   do per tal ven-   tu-ra tu- ta nu-
da   Fix'   a ba-gna-re el suo can-di- do vel-

que   Quan-   do per tal ven-tu-ra tu- ta nu-
da   Fix'   a ba- gna-re el suo can-di- do vel-

da   La
lo   C'al

da   La
lo   C'al

vi- di in me-ço de-le ge-lid' a-
so- le e l'au-ra el va-go ca-pel chiu-

vi-
so- di in me-ço de-le ge-lid' a-
le e l'au-ra el va-go ca-pel chiu-

[Ritornello]

que. 3. Tal che mi fi-ci quando'gl'ard' el cel-
da:

que. 3. Tal che me fi-ci quan- do 'gl' ard' el cel-
da.

lo, Tu- to tre-mar d'un a-mo- ro-so gel- lo.

lo, Tu- to tre-mar d'un a-mo- ro-so gel- lo.

50. Giovanni da Florentia (fl. c. 1350)

Nel mezzo

Madrigal

1. Nel
2. Et
3. Ma'l mez-zo a sei pa- on ne vi- di un bian-
quan-do puo mo- strar la suo bel- lez-
suo com- pa- gno sem-pre el va guar- dan-

co Con cre- sta d'o- ro e con mor-
za Ho- nor gli fa- cia- scun d'al-
do, E pur can- tan- do da lui

bi- tro da pen- na, Si
tro co- lo- re Per
non si par- Et

bel che dol- ce- men-te il cor mi spen-
la legg- ia- dra vi-sta, che ha, d'a-mo-
egl- i'l fa par- tir da se per ar-

53

51. Giovanni da Florentia

Io son un pellegrin

Ballata

54

52. Ghirardello da Firenze (fl. *c.* 1375)

Tosto che l'alba

Caccia

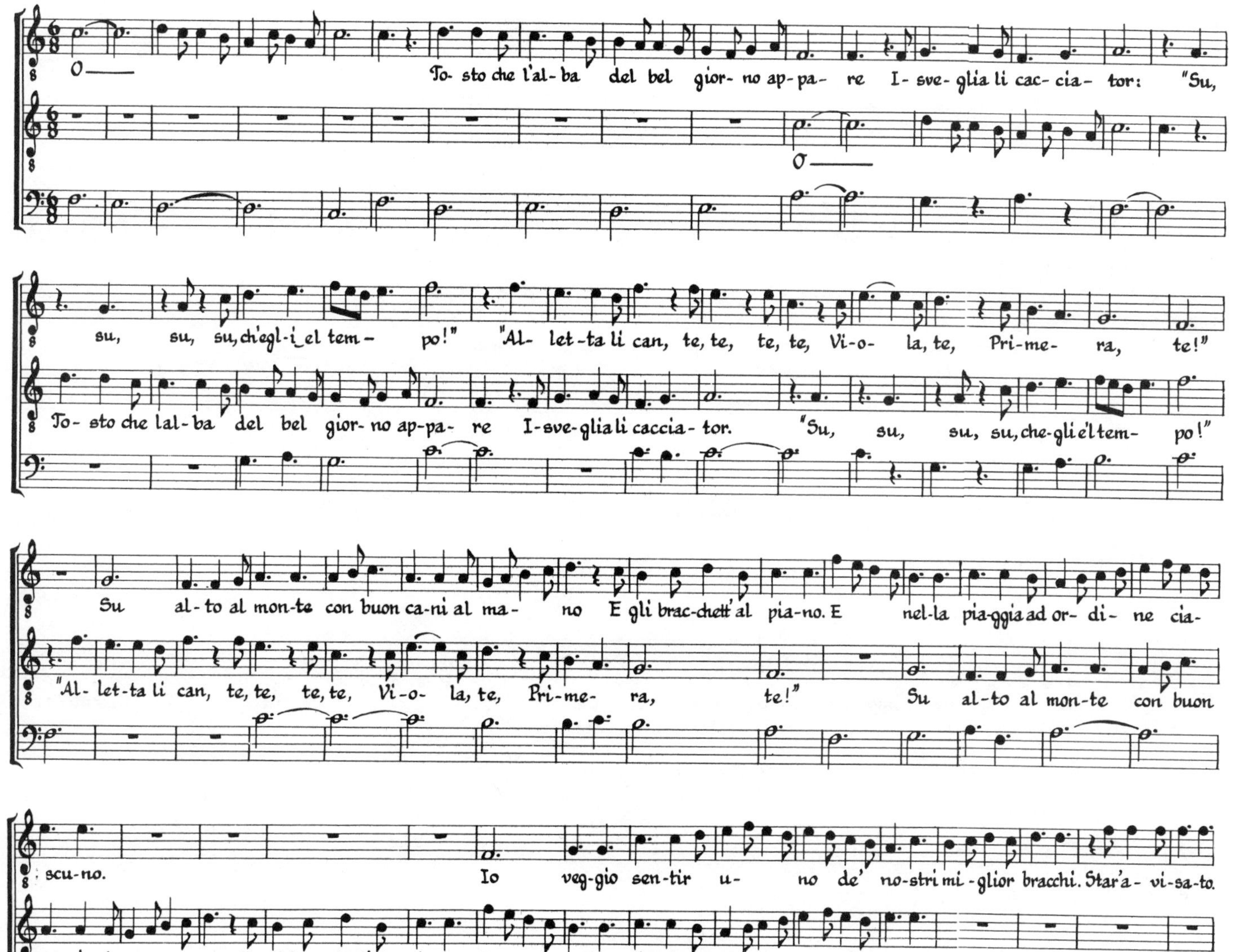

Ritornello

Del ... mon-te qué che v'e- ra su gri-da-va al al- tra all'

altre suo cor-no so-na-va ... mon-te que' che v'e- ra su gridava al al-tra all altre suo corno so-na-va

53. Francesco Landini (1325-1397)

Amor c'al tuo suggetto

Ballata

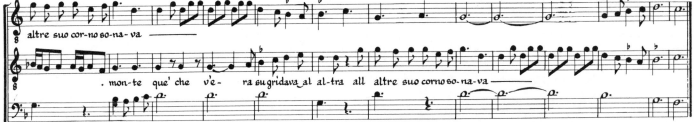

1.5. A- mor c'al tuo sug-get- to o- mai da lle- na. Sot- to
4. Per chè tut-ta vir-tu in lei si cre- a. O fe-

Contratenor

Tenor

(Fine)

tuo gio- go vi- vo san- ça pe- na.
li- ce cui le- ghi a ttal ca- te- na.

Secunda pars

2. Et co- si vo' con-ten- to sen- pre sta- re Po chè m'à
3. C'a nul- la co- sa si puo a- gua-glia- re Tal la pro-

56

54. Francesco Landini

Sy dolce non sono

Madrigal

58

facto fa contrario al gor-go—

ne.

Et

facto fa contrario al gor-go—

ne.

Et

facto fa contrario al gor-go—

ne.

55. Johannes Ciconia (fl. 1400)

Et in terra pax

Mass movement

Et in ter-ra pax ho-mi-ni-bus bo-nae vo-lun-ta-tis. 1. Lau-da— mus
Cr. 2. Qui tollis pec-ca-ta mun-

te. Be-ne-di-ci— mus te. Ad-o— ra-mus te. Glo-ri— fi-ca-mus te.
di, mi-se-re-re no-bis. Qui tol—lis peccata mun-di, sus-ci-pe de-preca-ti-o— nem no-stram.

Gra- ti-as a-gi-mus ti- bi prop- ter magnam gloriam tu-am, Do- mi- ne De-us, rex coele-stis, De-
Qui sedes ad dexte-ram Pa- tris, mi-se-re-re no- bis Quo-ni- am tu so-lus sanctus, tu

us pa-ter om-ni-potens. Do-mine fi-li u- ni-ge-ni-te Je- su Chri-ste. Do- mine De-us, a- gnus De- i,
so- lus Do- mi-nus, tu so- lus al-tis-si-mus Je-su Chri-ste, Cum Sancto Spiri- tu in glo-ri-

fi- li-us Pa— tris. A—
a De-i Pa— tris.

men.

56. Guillaume Legrant (fl. 1419)

Credo

57. School of Worcester (14th Century)

a. Alleluia psallat

Motet

b. Gloria in excelsis

Et in ter-ra pax ho-mi-ni-bus bo-ne vo-lun-ta-tis. Lau- da-mus te. Be-ne-di-ci-mus te. Ad-o-

ra-mus te. Glo-ri-fi-ca-mus te. Gra-ti-as a-gi-mus ti- bi propter magnam glo-ri-am tu- am, Do-mi-ne

De- us rex coe-le-stis De- us Pa- ter om-ni-po-tens. Do- mi-ne fi- li u- ni-ge-ni-

te Je-su Chri-ste. Do-mi-ne De-us, A-gnus De- i, fi- li- us Pa- tris.

58. Organ Estampie (*c.* 1325)

59. Italian Dances (14th Century)

a. Lamento di Tristan, with Rotta

Estampie

La Rotta

b. Saltarello

Estampie

60. Oswald von Wolkenstein (1377-1445)

Accompanied song

Der May

Der may mit lieber zal Die erd be-decket überal, Puhl, eben, perg und tal. Aus

süsser vogelein schal Erklin- gen, sin- gen hohen hal Ga- lander, lerchen, droschel, nachti- gal. Der gauch fleucht hinden

nach Mit grossem ungemach, Kleinen vogelein gogoleich. Ho- ret wie er sprach: cu-cu, cu-cu, Den zins gib mir, Den

wil ich han von dir Der hunger macht lunger Mir den Magen schier Ach elend nu wellent sol ich? So sprach das kleine

vieh. Kungel, zeisel, mays, lerch, nu kumm, wir sin- gen: sa und tu-ich tu-ich tu-ich tu-ich tu-ich, sa sa sa sa sa sa sa sa

sa sa sa sa, fi fideli fideli fideli fi, ci ci-e-ri-ri ci-ri ci-e-ri-ri ci-ri ci-ri ci-ri-li, sia sia so sing der

gauch nur ka-wa-wa, cu-cu. Ra-co so sprach der rab Zwar ich sing auch wol, Vol mus
ich sein Das sin-gen mein: Scheub ein, her-ein, vol sein. Liri li-ri li-ri li-ri li-ri li-ri-lon, So sang die lerch, so
sang die lerch, so sang die lerch. Ich sing hel ein drosch lein, ich sing hel ein droschlein, ich sing hel ein drosch lein, das in dem wald erklingt;
ir-lie-rent, zie-rent, grachet, grachet und wa-chet hin und her, recht als unser pha-rer. Zi-di-wick, zi-di-wick, zi-di-wick,
zi-si-ci-go, zi-si-ci-go, zi-si-ci-go, nachtigall, Die selb-mit irem ge-sang behub den grall. sang behub den grall.

IV. Early Fifteenth Century

61. John Dunstable (*c.* 1370-1453)

O rosa bella
Accompanied song

[instrumental]

O ro-sa bella, o dolce a-

Ct.

T.

62. John Dunstable

Sancta Maria

Hymn (motet)

63. Lionel Power (Early 15th Century)

Sanctus

Mass movement

64. Damett (Early 15th Century)

Beata Dei genitrix

Hymn

de pro de- vo- to fe- mi- ne- o se- xu, Al- le- lu- ya.

65. Guillaume Dufay (*c*. 1400-1474)

Alma redemptoris mater

Antiphon B.M.V.

Al- ma redemptoris ma- ter, quae pervi- a caeli por- ta ma- nes, Et stel- la ma- ris etc.

Al- ma re- demp- to- ris

Ma- ter, quae per- vi- a coe- li por- ta ma-

nes, Et stel- la ma-

ris, suc- cur- re ca- den- ti sur- ge- re qui cu- rat po- pu- lo. Tu

quae ge- nu- i- sti na- tu- ra mi- ran- te tuum san- ctum Ge-

66. Guillaume Dufay

a. L'Homme armé

L'homme, l'homme, l'homme ar- mé, l'homme ar- mé, L'homme ar- mé doibt on dou- ter. On a fait par-tout cri-

er Que chas- cun se viengue ar- mer D'un hau- bre-gon de fer.

b. Kyrie I

Missa L'Homme armé

c. Agnus Dei III

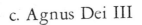

67. Guillaume Dufay

Mon chier amy

Ballade

[instru-mentall?]

1. Mon chier a- my qu'a-ves vous em- pen- se de ret- te- nir en vous me-ran-co- lie
2. Se dieur nous a un bon a- my e- ste et des-se- vre de vos- stre com-pa- gnie

re- te- me-ran- co- lie

3. Ne met-tes pas en a- ban-don la

la

vi- e Pri es pour luy lais-sies ce du-eil a- ler, Car u- ne

vie dueil a- ler

[instrumental?]

fois nous fault ce pas pas-ser.

68. Guillaume Dufay

Adieu m'amour

Rondeau

A

A- dieu m'a- mour, a- dieu ma ioy- e, A-dieu le so-las que i'a- voy-

Tenor
A- dieu m'a- mour, a- dieu ma ioy- e, A-dieu le so- las que i'a-voy-

Contratenor

69. Gilles Binchois (*c.* 1400-1467)

De plus en plus

Rondeau

70. Gilles Binchois

Files à marier

Chanson

ja]
Car se ja-lou-sie a   ja-lou-sie a   Ja-mais ne vous ne lui   [ja-

vous ma-ri-ez ja,   Car se ja-lou-sie a   ja-lou-sie a ja-   mais ne vous ne lui, ja-mai ne vous ne

mais] jamais ne vous ne lui   au cuer joy-e n'a-ra   joy-e n'a-ra,   [au cuer joy-e n'a-   ra.]

lui   au cuer joy-e n'a-ra   au cuer joy-e n'a-ra   joy-e n'a-ra [au cuer joy-e n'a-ra, au cuer joy-e n'a-ra]

71. Arnold de Lantins (fl. *c.* 1450)

Puisque je voy

Rondeau

1.4.7. Puis-que je voy bel-   le que ne   ma-   mes   Et que aul-tre que   moy a-ves
3. He-   las he   my ou   sont bien dif-   fa-   mes   Mes faits et sy n'ay   que dueil et
5. Rient mains je   croys quant   bien pen-se   a-   ves   Que vo-stre suy et   que vous ay

T.

Ct.

choy-   si   [instrumental?]
sou-   ssy.   2.8. Mon cuer cer-   tes   en est si
ser-   vy.   6. Vos nos ren-dres   vei-ant qu'a-

es-na-   vri   Que tous plai-sirs sont de soy de-bou-tes.   [instrumental?]
ves fal-   ly   Et que d'ain-sy fai-re rai-son n'a-ves.

72. Hugo de Lantins (fl. *c.* 1450)

Ce ieusse fait

Rondeau

V. Late Fifteenth Century

73. Johannes Ockeghem (1430-1495)

a. Kyrie

Missa L'Homme armé

b. Agnus Dei III

Missa L'Homme armé

74. Johannes Ockeghem

Ma maîtresse   Virelai

Ma bouche rit

Virelai

1.5. Ma bouche rit et ma pen-sé-e pleu— re, Mon œil s'es- joie et mon cueur mau-dit l'eu-
4. Vos-tre pi-tié veult douc-ques que je meu— re, Mais ri- gueur veult que vi- vant je de-meu—

Ct.

T.

re, Qu'il eust le bien qui sa san- té dé-chas- se, Et le plai- sir que la mort
re, Ain- si meurs vif, et en vi- vant trespas- se, Mais pour ce- ler le mal qui

me pour-chas- se Sans ré-con- fort qui m'ai-de ne se- queu—
ne se pas- se Et pour cou-vrir le deul ou je la-beu—

re.
re.

2. Ha, cueur per- vers, faul-saire et men-son- gier Dic- tes comment a- vez o- sé
3. Puis qu'en ce point vous vous vo- lez ven- gier, Pen- sez bien tost de ma vie a—

son-bre— gier, Que de faul-cer ce que m'a- vez pro- mis?
bre— gier, Vi- vre ne puis au point où m'a- vez mis.

76. Jacob Obrecht (1430-1505)

a. O beate Basili (prima pars)

Motet

b. O vos omnes

Motet

77. Jacob Obrecht

a. Kyrie I

Missa Sine nomine

78. Jacob Obrecht

Tsaat een meskin

Instrumental canzona

79. Loyset Compère (d. 1518)

Royne du ciel

Rondeau

Roy-ne du ciel qui du layt vir-gi-nal A-vez moil-

Roy-ne du ciel qui du layt vir-gi-nal A-vez moil-

Re-gi-na cae-li

lé du filz de dieu la fa-ce B Pré-ser-vez moy du

lé du filz de dieu la fa-ce Pré-ser-vez moy du lo-

Re-gina cae-li Re-gi-na

lo-gis in-fer-nal Car vous es-tez tré-so-riè-re de gra-

gis in-fer-nal Car vous es-tez tré-sp-riè-

cae-li Re-gi-na cae-li.

83

re de gra- ce. ce.

80. Heinrich Finck (1445-1527)

Veni sancte spiritus — Veni creator spiritus

Quodlibet

ve- ni, san- cte spi- ri- tus,
ve- ni cre- a- tor spi-

et e- mit- te coe- li- tus
ri- tus, men- tes tu- o- rum vi- si- ta, im- ple

lu- cis tu- ae ra- di- um,
su- per- na gra- ti- a, quae tu cre-

lu- cis tu- ae ra- di- um.
a- sti pe- cto- ra.

81. Conrad Paumann (1410-1473)

a. Mit ganczem Willen

Lochamer Liederbuch, c. 1450

(Instrumental)

Mit ganczem Willen wünsch ich dir Seind ich mich dir er- ge- ben han. In dei- nem g'pot fraw
Ob es ge- steht nach dein begier Will ich ge- waltig- li- chen stan.

vein on spot So bleib ich dein al- ley- ne Du al- ler- liebsts frew- lei- ne.

b. Mit ganczem Willen

Paumann's *Fundamentum Organisandi*, 1452

(Mit)

(Seind)

Repeticio

(Du)

82. Glogauer Liederbuch (*c.* 1460)

O rosa bella

O rosa bella   In feuers hitz so brennet mein herz   Ich sachs eins mals den lichten morgen- ster- ne

So, so, mein libste zart   O senens kraft   mit deinem haft   Zu aller zeit in ge- dan- kes gir.

85

83. Glogauer Liederbuch

a.

Instrumental piece

b. Der neue Bauernschwanz

For Instruments

84. Organ Preludes

a. Praeambulum in G Tablature of Adam Ileborgh, 1448

b. Praeambulum super D, A, F et G   Tablature of Adam Ileborgh

c. Praeambulum super G   Buxheim Organ Book, *c.* 1470

d. Praeambulum super C   Buxheim Organ Book

e. Praeambulum in mi

Tablature of Leonhard Kleber, 1524

f. Praeambulum in re

Tablature of Leonhard Kleber

g. Praeambulum in fa

Tablature of Hans Kotter, c. 1520

85. English Part Song, *c.* 1475

Tappster, Drinker

86. Two English Part Songs, c. 1500

a. A dew, a dew

Robert Cornysh (1465–1523)

b. I have been a foster

Cooper

VI. Early Sixteenth Century

87. Heinrich Isaac (c. 1450-1517)

Zwischen Berg und tiefem Tal

German part song

88. Heinrich Isaac

Instrumental canzona

89. Josquin des Près (1450-1521)

Agnus Dei "Ex una voce tres" (Mensuration canon)　　　　　　　　　Missa L'Homme armé

A- gnus　　Dei qui　tol-lis pecca- ta mun-　　di mi- miserere no-　　bis

90. Josquin des Près

Tu pauperum refugium　　　　　　　　　　　　　　　　　　　　　Motet

quo- rum re- me- di- um,

Tu pau-pe-rum re- fu- gi- um, tu lan-guo-　rum re-　me- di- um, spes ex- su- lum, for-

quo- rum re- me- di- um,

91. Josquin des Près

Faulte d'argent

Chanson

92. Pierre de la Rue (*c.* 1460-1518)

Kyrie I and II

Missa L'Homme armé

93. Paulus Hofhaimer (1459-1537)

Mein's traurens ist

German part song

96

94. Giacomo Fogliano (1473-1548)

Ave Maria

Lauda

95. Two Frottole

a. Non val aqua

Bartolomeo Tromboncino (fl. 1500)

(2) piu se rin-for-za, Quanto piu con quel mi sfo-co. Volta.
(5) co e co-me el pa-scie Che nel a- qua ha el pro- prio lo-co: 6. Non val a- qua al mio gran

fo-co, Che per pian-to non s'a-morza, Che per pian-to non s'a-morza, Che per pian-

to non s'a-mor- za.

b. In te Domine

Jusquin d'Ascanio (fl. 1500)

Ripresa. 1. In te, do-mi-ne, spe-ra- vi Per tro-var pie-
Piedi. 3. Rot-to e al ven-to o-gni spe-ran- za; Veg-gio il ciel vol-
4 Su-spir la-chry-me m'a-van- za. Del mio tri-sto

A.

(1) ta in e- ter- no, 2. Ma in un tri- sto e ob-scu- ro in-fer- no
(3) tar- mi in pian- to, 5. Fui fe- ri- to, se non quan- to
(4) spe- rar tan- to, B.

(2) Fui e fru-stra la- bo- ra- vi. Volta.
(5) Tri- bu-lan-do ad te cla-ma- vi: 6. In te, do- mi- ne,

spe- ra-vi. [In te do- mi- ne.]

96. Canto Carnascialesco (c. 1500)

Per scriptores

97. Millan (Late 15th Century)

a. Oh dulce

Villancico

de que yo go- zar so- li- a.

b. Durandarte Villancico

Duran-dar- te Du- randar- te, buen ca- ba- lle- ro pro- ba- do yo te

Fine

rue- go que ha- ble- mos en a quel tiem- po pa- sa- do.

Da capo

98. Juan Encina (1469-c. 1530)

a. Congoxa mas Villancico

Fine

A.
1. Con- go- xa mas que cru- el ve- vir, Comba- te, mi tri- ste vi- da,
4. Es fan tris- te mi que se- rá me- jor mo- rir: La causa fué mi par- ti- da.

B.
2. Par- tir- me sin me par- sen- tir- da,
3. De vos, gra- cio- sa y

Da capo al Fine

b. Pues que jamás Villancico

A.
1. Pues que ja- más ol- vi- da- ros No pue- de mi corazon Si me fal- ta ga- lardon
4. Mas si vos, por bien a- ma- ros, Que- reis darme galardon, No di- ra mi co- razon

Fine B.
¡Ay, que mal hice en mira- ros! 2. Sera tal vis- ta cobrar Gran do- lor y gran tris- tu- ra.
¡Ay, que mal hice en a- ma- ros! 3. Sera tal vis- ta penar, Si me fa- llece ven- tu- ra.

Da capo al Fine

c. Mas vale trocar

99. Two Lute Ricercars (c. 1500)

a. Tastar de corde con il ricercar dietro

Joanambrosio Dalza

b. Ricercar

Francesco Spinaccino

100. Arnolt Schlick (d. after 1517)

Salve Regina

Organ hymn

Sal- ve, Re- gi- na, mater mi- se- ri- cor- di- ae.

101

orig: c c dd

101. Arnolt Schlick

Maria zart   Organ hymn

102. Two Dances

a. Alta

F. de la Torre (*c.* 1500)

b. Spanyöler Tancz   Hans Weck (*c.* 1510)

Hopper dancz

103. English Dompe (c. 1525)

My Lady Carey's Dompe

For Harpsichord

da capo from § (suggested close)

105

104. French Pavane (1530)

For Harpsichord

105. Hans Neusiedler (1508-1563)

a. Hoftanz

Lute dance

Der Hupf auff

b. Der Juden Tanz

106. Antoine de Fevin (1437-c.1515)

Missa Mente tota

Agnus Dei

107. Clement Janequin (1485-c. 1560)

L'Alouette

Program chanson

108. Thomas Stoltzer (c. 1480-1526)

Christ ist erstanden

German hymn

109. Ludwig Senfl (c. 1490-c. 1550)

Salutatio prima

110. Ludwig Sénfl

Da Jakob nu das Kleid ansah

111. Two Settings of a German Chorale

a. Aus tiefer Not

Johann Walter (1496–1570)

b. Aus tiefer Not

Arnold von Bruck (c. 1500–1554)

112. John Taverner (c. 1495–1545)

a. The Western Wynde

b. Benedictus

Mass The Western Wynde

113. Adrian Willaert (*c.* 1485-1562)

Victimae paschali laudes

Motet

116

114. Nikolaus Gombert (d. *c.* 1560)

Super flumina

Motet

115. Adrian Willaert

Ricercar

For Instruments

116. Girolamo Cavazzoni (b. c. 1515)

Ricercar

For Organ

117. Girolamo Cavazzoni

Missa Apostolorum (Cunctipotens)

Organ Mass

Chyrie primus Ky-ri- e   e-   le-i-son.

Christe Chri-ste   e-   le-i-son.

Chirie quartus

Et in terra pax

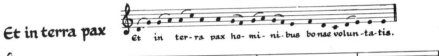

Benedicimus te

Glorificamus te

Domine Deus, Rex

Do-mi-ne De-us, Rex coe-le-stis, De- us Pa- ter om-ni-po-tens.

Domine Deus, Agnus Dei

Do-mi ne De-us, A-gnus De-i , Fi- li-us Pa- tris

Qui tollis

Qui tol-lis peccata mundi, susci-pe deprecatio- nem nostram.

125

Quoniam — Quo-ni-am tu solus sanctus.

Tu solus altissimus — Tu solus Altissi-mus, Je- su Chri-   ste.

Amen — A— men.

118. Girolamo Cavazzoni

Falte d'argens

Organ canzona

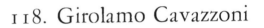

119. Silvestro Ganassi (b. 1492)

Two Ricercars

For Viola da gamba

120. John Redford (1485-1545)

a. Veni redemptor

Organ hymn

Ve- ni re-demptor gen-ti-um, os-ten-de par-tum vir-gi-nis, mi-re-tur om-ne se-cu-lum, ta-lis de-cet par-tus de-um.

(Veni)

(ostende)

(mi retur)

(x)

(talis)

b. Lucem tuam

Organ hymn

128

121. Luis de Milan (fl. 1535)

Fantasia

For Lute

122. Luis de Narvaez (fl. 1538)

Diferencias sobra O Gloriosa Domina

Variations for Lute

Quarta diferencia de proporcion.

Quinta diferencia. El canto llano por tiple.

Sesta diferencia. El canto llano por tenor.

123. Miguel de Fuenllana (fl. 1554)

Paseábase el rey

Lute song

Voice

Pa- se- á- ba- se el rey

Lute

mo- ro   Por   la   ciu- dad   de   Gra- na- da.   Car-

tas   le   fue- ron   ve- ni-   das

Co- mo Al- ha- ma   e- ra ga- na- da.   Ay!   mi Al-   ha-

124. Anriquez de Valderravano (fl. 1547)

Diferencias sobre Guardame las vacas

Variations for Lute

125. Clemens Non Papa (c. 1510-c. 1555)

Vox in Rama

Motet

126. Two Settings of Psalm 35

a. Deba contre mes debateurs

Claude Goudimel (c. 1505–1572)

b. Deba contre mes debateurs

Claude le Jeune (1528–1600)

136

127. Thomas Tallis (c. 1505-1585)

Audivi vocem

Responsorium

137

128. Cristobal Morales (*c.* 1500-1553)

Emendemus in melius

Motet

129. Costanzo Festa (d. 1545)

Quando ritrova   Madrigal

130. Iacob Arcadelt (*c.* 1514-after 1557)

Voi ve n'andat' al cielo

Madrigal

131. Cipriano de Rore (1516–after 1557)

Da le belle contrade

Madrigal

132. Louis Bourgeois (c. 1510–after 1561)

Qui au conseil

Psalm 1

133. Antonio de Cabezon (1510–1566)

Versos del sexto tono

Organ verses

144

3. Tenor canto llano

4. Contrabaxo canto llano

134. Antonio de Cabezon

Diferencias Cavallero

Variations

(1)

(2)

(3)

135. Andrea Gabrieli (1510-1586)

Intonazione settimo tono

Organ prelude

136. Andrea Gabrieli

"Ricercare del 12° tono"   Instrumental canzona

147

137. Claude Gervaise (fl. 1550)

Three Dances

For Instruments

1 Basse danse La Volunté

[Fine]

[Da capo al fine]

2. Pavane d'Angleterre

Gaillarde

3. Allemande

138. Claude le Jeune (1528-1600)

D'une coline

Vers mesuré

Dessus

Cinquiesme

Taille

Dú-ne co- li-ne my prou-me-nant Par la plu vert' et plu gay- e sai-zon Quand tou-te cho- se rid au chams, Je voy

u- ne Rô- ze ver-meil-lé-te Qui tou-te fleu-ré-te de fleur de beau-té Pas- se de bien loin.

Rechant à 3

Je la voy de loin,

Et je l'ai- me fort, Je la veu cueil-lir, Et la main j'y tens, Mais las c'est en vain.

Reprise à 5

Dessus

Cinquiesme

Je la voy de loin, Et je l'ai- me fort, Je la veu cuil-lir, Et la main j'y tens, Mais las c'est en vain.

Haut Contre

Taille

Basse Contre

139. Francisco Guerrero (1528-1599)

Salve Regina

Antiphon B.M.V.

VII. Late Sixteenth Century

140. Giovanni Palestrina (1525-1594)

Agnus Dei I

Missa Papae Marcelli

141. Giovanni Palestrina

Sicut cervus

Motet

153

154

Alla riva del Tebro

Madrigal

143. Orlando di Lasso (1532-1594)

Introit: Requiem aeternam

Missa Pro defunctis

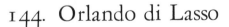

144. Orlando di Lasso

Penitential Psalm III, v. 1, 10, 20

1.

10.

20.

145. Orlando di Lasso

a. Bon jour, mon coeur

Chanson

b. Bon jour, mon coeur

Keyboard arrangement by Peter Philips (*c.* 1560 – after 1633)

146. Madrigal with Parody Mass

a. Cara la vita (Madrigal)

Jacob van Werth (1536–1596)

b. Missa super Cara la vita (Parody Mass)

Philipp de Monte (1521–1603)

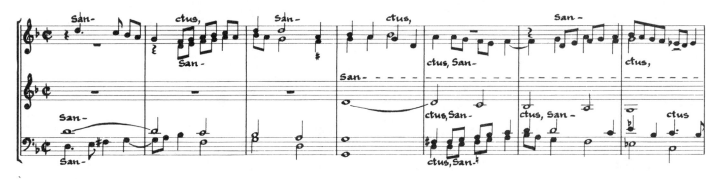

147. Guillaume Costeley (1531-1606)

Chanson

Allon, gay, gay

148. Jacobus de Kerle (1531-1591)

Exurge, Domine

Motet

149. Tomas Luis de Victoria (c. 1540-1611)

O vos omnes

Motet

150. William Byrd (1543-1623)

Non vos relinquam

Motet

151. William Byrd

Verse anthem

Christ rising again

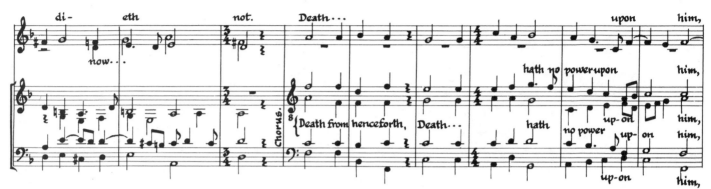

152. Giovanni Maria Nanini (c. 1545-1607)

Hic est beatissimus

Motet

teris al-ti-us a Domino me-ru-it ho-no-ra-ri, me-ru-it ho-no-ra-ri, me-
al-ti-us a Do-mi-no me-ru-it ho-no-
teris al-ti-us a Do-mi-no me-ruit ho-no-ra-ri, me-ru-it ho-no-ra-ri,

ru-it ho-no-ra-ri.
ra-ri.
me-ru-it ho-no-ra-ri.

153. Claudio Merulo (1533-1604)

Toccata

154. Passamezzo antico

a.

Nicolaus Ammerbach (c. 1530–1597)

La Reprisa

Saltarello

b.

Giovanni Picchi (fl. 1600–1620)

Seconda Parte

Quarta Parte

Follow 2 more variations.

155. Luca Marenzio (*c.* 1560-1599)

Madonna mia gentil

Madrigal

156. Jacob Handl (1550-1591)

Ecce quomodo

Motet

In ecclesiis

Motet with Organ and Instruments

158. Giovanni Gastoldi (*c.* 1556-1622)

L'Acceso

Balletto

Più d'ogn' al-tro Clo-ri Tu sei bel-la e va-ga E'l tuo vis'ogn' alm' ap-pa-ga Fa la la...

Più...

Più...

159. Thomas Morley (1557-1603)

My bonny lass

Ballett

160. Felice Anerio (1560-1614)

a. Al suon

Song

b. Al suon

For Harpsichord and Lute

161. Carlo Gesualdo (*c.* 1560-1614)

Io pur respiro

Madrigal

162. John Danyel (*c.* 1565-1630)

Stay, cruel, stay

Ayre with Lute and Viola da gamba

spect, O seeme but to re- spect mee. Yet say farewel, spect mee.

163. John Dowland (1563-1626)

a. What if I never speed
Ayre (choral)

can no loss
can command

1. What if I nev-er speed, Shall I straight yield to des- pair And still on sorrow feed That can no loss re- pair?
2. Or shall I change my love, For I find power to de- part, And in my reason prove That I can command my heart?

still on sor- row
in my rea- son

still on sorrow feed
in my reason prove

But if she will pi- ty my de-sire and my love re- quite, Then ev-er shall she live my dear de-

But if she will pi- ty, pi-ty, pi-ty my de-sire and my love re-quite,

But if she will pi- ty my desire and my love, my love re-quite Then evershall she live my dear de- light,

But if she will pi-ty my de-sire and my love re-quite, Then...

light. Come, come, come, while I have a heart to de- sire thee, Come, come, come,

Come, come, come, while I have a heart to de- sire thee, Come, come,

Come, come, come, while I have a heart to de- sire thee, Come, come,

Come, come, come, while I have a heart to de- sire thee, Come, come,

for ei- ther I will love or ad- mire thee.

for ei-ther I will love or ad- mire thee.

for ei- ther I will love or ad-mire thee.

for ei- ther I will love or ad- mire thee.

1. What if I nev-er speed,
2. Or shall I change my

love, Shall I straight yield to des- pair And
love, For I find power to de- part, And

still on sor- row feed
in my rea- son prove

That I can no loss re- pair?
I can com- mand my heart?

But if she will pi-ty my de-sire and my love re-quite, Then e-ver shall she live my dear de-light, Come,

Come, come, while I have a heart to de-sire thee, Come, come, come for ei-ther I will love or ad-mire thee.

164. Hans Leo Hassler (1564-1612)

Quia vidisti me

Motet

Qui-a vi-di-sti me, Thoma, cre- di-di- sti, vi-di sti me, Tho-ma, qui- a vi-

Qui- a vi di sti me, Thoma, cre-di-di- sti, vi- -di- di- sti, qui-sti,

Qui-a vi-di-sti me, Thoma, cre- di-di- sti,

Qui- a vi-di-sti me, Tho-ma, cre- di-di- sti,

di-sti me, Thoma, credi-di- sti, vi-di-sti me, Tho- ma, cre-di-di- sti, be-a- ti, be-

a... qui- a... cre- di-di- sti, Tho- ma, credi-di- sti; be-a- ti, be-a- ti, be-

Tho- ma, credi-di- sti; be-a- ti, be-a- ti, be-

qui- a... cre- di-di- sti, be- a- ti, be-

186

165. Hans Leo Hassler

Ach Schatz   Lied

Tu freundlich mit mir scherzen, Verkehr, verkehr in freud mein schmerzen, Sonst...

auf-ge-ben, mein geist auf-ge-ben.

166. Gregor Aichinger (1564-1628)

Factus est
Motet

167. Michael Praetorius (1571-1621)

a. Vater unser im Himmelreich

Chorale bicinium

b. Ballet du Roy pour sonner après

Instrumental suite

168. Melchior Franck (*c.* 1573 - 1639)

So wünsch ich ihr

Lied

169. Thomas Tomkins (1573-1636)

When David heard

Anthem

lom my son, O my son, Ab- sa- lom my son.

son,
Ab- sa- lom my son, O Ab- sa- lom my son, O Ab- sa- lom, Ab- sa- lom my son.

O Ab- sa- lom my son, O Ab- sa- lom my son, my son.

son,

O Ab- sa- lom my son.

170. Thomas Weelkes (c. 1575-1623)

Hark, all ye lovely saints

Ballett

Hark all ye love-ly saints a-bove, Di- an- a hath a- greed with love, hath a-greed with love, his

Hark all ye love-ly saints a-bove, Di- an- a hath a- greed with love, hath a-greed with love, his

Di- an- a hath a- greed...

to re- move. Fa la la la la la la la la

fi- ery wea-pon to re- move, Fa la la la la la la...

fi- ery wea-pon to re- move. Fa la la la la la... Fa la la la la la... Fa la...

Fa la la la la la la... Fa la...

la. Fa la... 1. Hark 2. la.

Do you not see how they a-gree? Then

Fa la... la. Hark la.

la. Hark la. Do you not see how they a-gree? Then
la. Hark la.

la. Hark la.

193

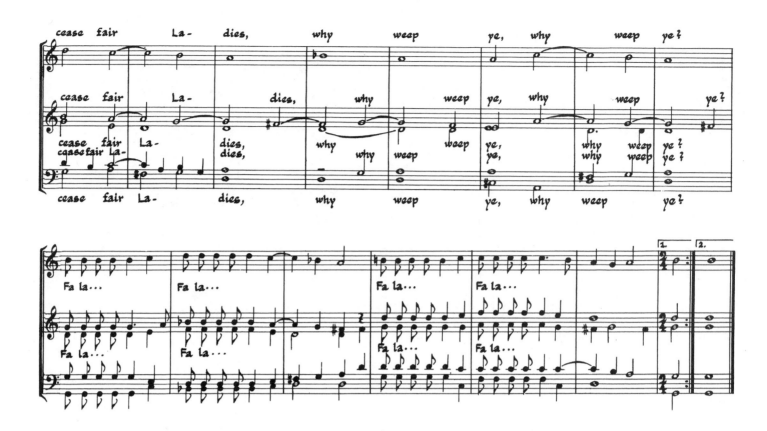

171. Orlando Gibbons (1583-1625)

O Lord, increase my faith

Anthem

172. Orlando Gibbons

This is the record of John

Verse Anthem

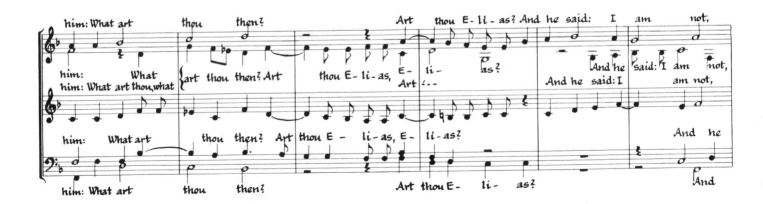

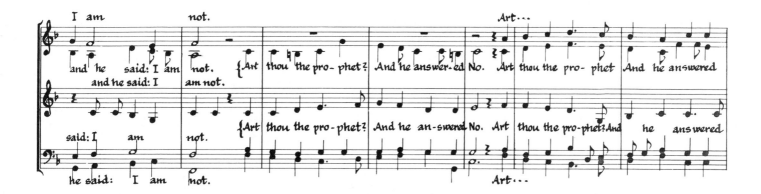

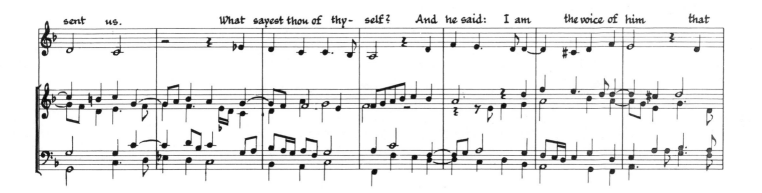

197

173. Giovanni Gabrieli

Sonata pian' e forte

For Instruments

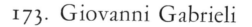

174. Giovanni Macque (fl. 1584-1613)

Consonanze stravaganti

For Organ

175. Florentio Maschera (1540-1584)

Canzona

For Instruments

176. Thomas Tomkins (1573-1656)

In Nomine

For Instruments

177. John Munday (d. 1630)

Goe from my window   Harpsichord variations

178. John Bull (1563 - 1628)

Praeludium

For Harpsichord

179. Orlando Gibbons

Pavane Lord Salisbury

For Harpsichord

The Galliard

180. Jean Titelouze (1563-1633)

Pange lingua

Organ hymn

181. Jan Pieterszon Sweelinck (1562-1621)

Fantasia in echo

For Organ

COMMENTARY

ABBREVIATIONS

AdHM · G. Adler, *Handbuch der Musikgeschichte*, 2 vols., 1930
ApNPM · W. Apel, *Notation of Polyphonic Music*, Third Edition, 1945
AR · *Antiphonale Sacrosanctae Romanae Ecclesiae*, 1924 (No. 820)
AS · *L'Anthologie Sonore*
Ba · Codex Bamberg *Ed. IV. 6*, ed. by P. Aubry, *Cent Motets du XIIIe siècle*, 3 vols., 1908
DdT · *Denkmäler deutscher Tonkunst*, 65 vols., 1892–1931
DTB · *Denkmäler der Tonkunst in Bayern*, 36 vols., 1900–1913
DTOe · *Denkmäler der Tonkunst in Oesterreich*, 83 vols., 1894–1938
ExMM · H. Expert, *Les Maîtres musiciens de la renaissance française*
F · Codex Florence, Bibl. Laur. *plut. 29.1*
GSE · *The Gramophone Shop Encyclopedia of Recorded Music*, 1942
LU · *Liber Usualis Missae et Officii*, 1937 (No. 780)
Mo · Codex Montpellier, Fac. des Méd. *H 196*, ed. by Y. Rokseth, *Polyphonies du XIIIe siècle*, 4 vols., 1936–39
ReMMA · G. Reese, *Music in the Middle Ages*, 1940
W₁ · Codex Wolfenbüttel *677* (facsimile edition by J. H. Baxter, *An Old St. Andrews Music Book*, 1931)
W₂ · Codex Wolfenbüttel *1206*

NOTE. The source references indicate either the original source of the composition or a modern reprint, depending upon which of these has been used. Reference to records is made on the basis of the Columbia, Decca, and Victor catalogues, *L'Anthologie Sonore,* and *The Gramophone Shop Encyclopedia of Recorded Music* (1942).

1. CHINESE. The Entrance Hymn for the Emperor formed a part of the ancient tradition of the Chinese court ceremonial, a tradition which dates back perhaps more than one thousand years before Christ. In the period of the Tang dynasty (A.D. 618–907) such "instrumental hymns" were performed by large orchestras, consisting of 120 zithers (*ch'in*), 180 lutes (*p'ip'a*), 200 mouth organs (*sheng*), 20 oboes, and numerous drums, bells, and chimes. The melodies of both the ancient hymn and the modern instrumental piece are written in the traditional five-tone scale (pentatonic scale) of Chinese music; in this scale the third and seventh degrees of the diatonic scale are omitted, and hence there are no semitones. ¶ Sources: (a) J. A. van Aalst, *Chinese Music* (1884, 1933), p. 26; (b) E. Fischer, in *Sammelbände der Internationalen Musikgesellschaft*, XII, 189.

2. JAPANESE. This composition affords a good example of heterophonic accompaniment, that is, a style in which the same melody is followed by all the performers with slight modifications. The *so* (or *koto*) is an oblong zither, derived from the Chinese *ch'in*. The dissonant anticipations, as in measure 8, are typical of Japanese music. The melody of this piece, like the Chinese melodies, is pentatonic, but the scale used here includes a semitone: e-f-a-b-d′-e′. The frequent use of the descending motif b-a-f-e (or e′-d′-b-a) may be noticed. ¶ Source: *Tōkyō Ongaku Gakkō, Sōkyokushū (Tokyo School of Music, Songs Accompanied by the So)*, II, 29.

3. SIAMESE. The regional rulers of Siam (and of Java) maintain fairly large orchestras, probably descended from those of ancient China. All the instruments play the same melody with certain variants (heterophonic accompaniment). The whole composition sounds an octave higher than written. The tempo gradually increases from M.84 to M.136. ¶ Source: C. Stumpf, "Tonsystem der Siamesen," *Beiträge zur Akustik und Musikwissenschaft,* vol. III (1901), Beilage.

4. HINDU. This chant (*sāman* = chant) is from the Sāmaveda, a body of religious texts dating back to about 1000 B.C. The first melody here given (1), transcribed from the Hindu notation, is perhaps just as old as the text. The second version (2) gives the same chant as sung today, transcribed from a phonographic recording. ¶ Sources: (1) R. Simon, in *Wiener Zeitschrift für die Kunde des Morgenlandes*, XXVII (1913), 318; (2) E. Felber, in *Sitzungsberichte der Kaiserlichen Akademie der Wissenschaften Wien*, Phil.-Hist. Klasse, Band 170, Abhandlung 7 (1912), p. 101.

5. ARABIAN. This example illustrates the popular music of the Arabians, as practiced in the towns of Tunisia. It is a

song accompanied by the *bendir* (*bandar*), a tambourine provided with a snare, and the *zukra* (*zûqqara*), a bagpipe with two chanters. A piece of Arabian music is invariably composed in a given *maqam,* a term which is frequently translated "mode." Actually, a maqam prescribes not only a scale (as do our church modes) but also the use of traditional motives, ornaments, etc. The present example shows, first, the scale of the maqam Hâsin sabâ; then an "Introductory Model" which serves to establish the maqam; and finally the song itself. ¶ Source: R. Lachmann, "Musik in den tunisischen Städten," *Archiv für Musikwissenschaft,* vol. v, Notenbeilage Nr. 4 and 5.

6. JEWISH. The first example (a) shows some of the notational signs of ancient Jewish music, *ta'amim* (so-called accents), with their rendition according to the Syrian rite. The second example (b) shows the intonation pattern used in reading from the Pentateuch, according to the Syrian rite. It consists, not of a freely invented melody, but of a succession of stereotyped motives represented by ta'amim. The tone C is a quarter-tone lower than in our scale. The third example (c) shows the beginning of Psalm 144 as sung in four different localities. The Ashkenazic (North European) versions show the influence of European musical style. ¶ Sources: (a) A. Z. Idelsohn, *Gesänge der babylonischen Juden* (1922), p. 44, no. 4; (b) *ibid.,* p. 34; (c) *ibid.,* p. 75ff.

7. GREEK. The First Delphic Hymn (No. 7a), dating from about 138 b.c., is the most considerable example of Greek music known. Only the first two sections are reproduced here, the third being incomplete. The first section (A) is in the Dorian octave species, normally e to e' (an ambitus corresponding to that of the Phrygian church mode), but transposed a whole tone upwards, f-sharp to f'-sharp, with b as the center tone (*mese*). To this tonality that of the second section (B) offers a striking contrast, owing to the extensive use of chromatic progressions. Quintuple rhythm, known as cretic meter, played an important part in Greek music. The Hymn to the Sun (No. 7b) is ascribed to Mesomedes of Crete, who lived about A.D. 130. The Song of Seikilos (No. 7c), dated variously from the second century B.C. to the first century A.D., is in the Phrygian octave species, d to d' (corresponding to the Dorian church mode), transposed a tone upwards. ¶ Sources: (a) Th. Reinach, *La Musique grecque* (1926), p. 177; (b) *ibid.,* p. 196, (c) *ibid.,* p. 193. ¶ Records: (a) *MSS-54* (*ReMMA,* p. 465); (b) and (c) *Decca 20156.*

8. BYZANTINE CHANT. These examples illustrate the liturgical music of the Byzantine Empire (founded A.D. 328; destroyed in 1453). While the rhythmic rendition of Gregorian chant has to the present day remained a subject of debate, that of Byzantine chant (at least, of the so-called Middle Period, *c.* 1100–1450) has been clarified in all its details. Octoechos (eight modes) is the name of books in which hymns for the daily offices are arranged according to the eight modes of the Byzantine Church which correspond to the eight modes of the Roman Church. ¶ Source: H. J. W. Tillyard, "Mediaeval Byzantine Music," *Musical Quarterly,* XXIII, 206 and 208, where most of the examples are incorrectly titled.

9. AMBROSIAN HYMNS. St. Ambrose (d. 397), bishop of Milan, is the most important figure in the early development of Latin hymnody. To what extent the melodies for his hymns represent an Ambrosian tradition is uncertain. In some cases the same text appears provided with a number of different melodies dating from various periods. Example 9a shows three different melodies (twelfth to fourteenth centuries) for "Aeterne rerum conditor." Example 9b shows the melody for "Aeterna Christi munera" in two rhythmic versions, (1) as notated in the ninth century *Musica enchiriadis;* (2) in what is frequently assumed to be the original form of the Ambrosian hymns, a reconstruction based on St. Augustine's remark that they were *tria temporum* (in three beats). The Ambrosian hymns, which form only a small division of the entire Ambrosian chant, are syllabic, in contrast to the remainder of the chant. ¶ Sources: (a) (1) H. Riemann, *Handbuch der Musikgeschichte,* 1.2, p. 17; (2) P. Wagner, *Neumenkunde* (1905, 1912), p. 239; (3) *AR,* p. 6. (b) (1) Gerbert, *Scriptores . . .* 1, 154; (2) cf. *AdHM,* p. 80.

10. AMBROSIAN CHANT. That branch of Christian chant which according to tradition was founded by St. Ambrose, and which is still in use today at the cathedral of Milan (therefore also known as Milanese chant). The melodies of this chant are considerably more melismatic than those of Gregorian (Roman) chant. The present example shows the verse of the gradual (called *psalmellus* in the Ambrosian rite) "Speciosus forma," (1) in the Ambrosian and (2) in the Gregorian version. ¶ Sources: (1) *Paléographie musicale,* VI, 86; (2) *LU,* p. 434.

11. GREGORIAN CHANT. Antiphon and psalm. This example illustrates the Gregorian method of psalm singing. The verses of the psalm are sung to a recitation melody (psalm tone) which consists of a reciting note called *tenor* and a number of short inflections called *initium* (intonation), *flexa* (flex), *mediatio* (mediation), and *terminatio* (cadence). The intonation is used for the first verse only, the flex only for longer verses which are divided into three sections instead of the usual two, for which mediation and cadence only are used. The doxology "Gloria Patri" is invariably added as a final verse of the psalm. The psalm is preceded and followed by an antiphon, in the present case "Laudabo Deum meum in vita mea." Before the psalm the antiphon is usually reduced to its first word (here, "Laudabo"), being sung in full only after the psalm. ¶ Source: *AR,* p. 127.

12. GREGORIAN CHANT: Gradual. The gradual is the second of the five items of the Proper of the Mass. It consists of two sections, the response ("Haec dies . . .") and the verse ("Confitemini . . ."). The response is sung by the chorus, except for the solo beginning, and the verse is sung

by the soloist or soloists, except for the choral close, as indicated by the asterisks in the text. The resulting manner of performance, an alternation between the soloists and the choir, attains particular importance in the polyphonic compositions of the graduals and similar chants (see Nos. 26ff). The present gradual is taken from the Mass for Easter Sunday. See also Nos. 29, 30, 31, 32. ¶Source: *LU*, p. 778. ¶Record: *GSE*, p. 201.

13. GREGORIAN CHANT: Alleluia. The alleluia is the third item of the Proper of the Mass. Its form (and manner of performance) is similar to that of the gradual. The melody for the response ("Alleluia") usually recurs at the end of the verse. The present example belongs to the Mass for Easter Monday. See also No. 26c. ¶Source: *LU*, p. 786.

14. GREGORIAN CHANT: Responsorium. The present selection is an example of the *responsoria prolixa,* as they are called in distinction from the much shorter *responsoria brevia.* The former are elaborate chants sung at Matins or Nocturns of high feasts (Christmas, Easter) and on a few other occasions. The "Libera me," which is sung at the Burial Service, is interesting because it illustrates the early, full form of responsorial singing in which a choral refrain, the response, alternates with various verses sung by the soloists, thus leading to a structure similar to that of the modern rondo as used in the final movements of sonatas or concertos. The form of the "Libera me" is as follows: R V_1 R' V_2 R" V_3 R. Here V_1, V_2, and V_3 are the verses *Tremens, Dies,* and *Requiem;* R is the response *Libera me,* R' and R" are sections thereof. ¶Source: *LU*, p. 1767.

15. GREGORIAN CHANT: Kyrie and Kyrie-trope. The Kyrie is the first item of the Ordinary of the Mass. Trope is the generic term for textual additions to the authorized texts as they were set down by Pope Gregory I. The present example of the Kyrie (a) is from the Mass IV, also known as *Missa Cunctipotens (cunctipotens = omnipotens)* or *Missa Apostolorum.* The former name refers to the trope here given (b) for the Kyrie of this Mass, a Latin poem ascribed to Tuotilo of St. Gall (d. *c.* 915) and sung in syllabic style to the melody of the (melismatic) Kyrie. ¶Sources: (a) *LU*, p. 25; (b) A. Schubiger, *Die Sängerschule von St. Gallen* (1858), p. 40.

16. SEQUENCES. The sequences are the oldest and most important type of tropes. They are accretions to the alleluias, and therefore can be described as alleluia tropes. Textually they are long poems, usually in the form a, b b, c c, . . . i i, k; that is, they begin and end with a single line (a, k) and in between there are a number of double-line stanzas. Musically, the relationship of the sequence melodies to those of the alleluias is by no means as clear and simple as it is frequently thought to be. Example 16a is one of the few sequences whose melody can be traced back to some extent to that of an alleluia. It is ascribed to Notker Balbulus of St. Gall, who died in 912. Example 16b is the Easter Sequence by Wipo (*c.* 1000–1050), one of the five sequences which are

still in use today. Example 16c represents a later type, the rhymed sequence. This usually has double-line stanzas (double versicles) all the way through. It was introduced by Adam of St. Victor (d. 1192), who wrote and composed a great number of such sequences in a style of formalistic elegance. The common French name for sequence is *prose,* probably an abbreviation of *pro s[equenti]a.* ¶Sources: (a) *LU*, p. 848, and Schubiger, *Die Sängerschule von St. Gallen,* p. 21; (b) *LU*, p. 780; (c) P. Aubry and E. Misset, *Les Proses d'Adam de St. Victor* (1900), p. 238.

17. LATIN LYRICS. The Latin lyric poetry of the twelfth and thirteenth centuries is known under the name of conductus. Examples 17a-d represent the monophonic conductus which, of course, preceded the polyphonic conductus exemplified by No. 38 and No. 39 of this collection. The *Conductus ad tabulam* (17a), widely known as the "Song of the Ass," belongs to the popular sphere. It formed the central part of a liturgical play at Beauvais during which the Virgin Mary was shown riding on an ass into the cathedral. Of the seven stanzas of the text, the first, fourth, and seventh are given here. Example 17b is a *rondellus,* that is, a conductus in the form of the medieval rondeau: a a a b a b, a form which figures prominently in the secular music of the thirteenth to the fifteenth centuries (cf. No. 19d-e). Examples 17c and 17d illustrate a more elaborate type of conductus melody, employing extended melismas (*copula, cauda*). Our rhythmic rendition of these songs is meant to bring out that peculiar mixture of metrical and non-metrical elements which, in the opinion of the editors, comes much closer to their true rhythm than the current interpretation in modal meter (triple time), which is here indicated in small notes (cf. F. Ludwig, in *AdHM*, p. 187). ¶Sources: (a) G. M. Dreves, *Analecta hymnica,* xx, 217, 257, and H. C. Greene, in *Speculum,* vol. VI; (b) Dreves, XXI, 213; (c) Codex Wolfenbüttel *1206* (W_2), fol. 156v; (d) Codex Florence, Bibl. Laur. *plut. 29.1* (*F*), fol. 422r. ¶Record: (c) *GSE*, p. 343.

18. TROUBADOURS. The troubadours were aristocratic poet-musicians of southern France (Provence) who, about 1100, inaugurated the first great flowering of secular music. They were followed about 1150 by the trouvères and the minnesingers. The troubadour melodies frequently suggest a more or less free rhythmic style (cf. the explanations under No. 17). The alternative versions given in No. 18c (1: Anglès; 2: Gérold; 3: Besseler) show that even within the limitations of modal rhythm various interpretations are possible, and that scholars are not in agreement regarding the details of its application. Marcabru's "Pax in nomine" (18a), said to have been composed in 1147, is an example of the *vers,* that is, of a through-composed song. Numbers 18b and 18c are examples of the *canzo,* showing the form a a b, which recurs in the trouvère *ballade* and in the *Bar* of the minnesingers and mastersingers. Number 18d is an *estampie,* a type of music which properly belongs to the instrumental field (see Nos. 40, 41). In fact, an old report tells us that Raimbault

wrote the words of "Kalenda maya" to a melody which two "joglar de Fransa" (jongleurs from northern France) performed on viols at the court of Montferrat. ¶ Sources: (a) *Tribune de St. Gervais*, x, 113ff; (b) C. Appel, *Die Singweisen des Bernart de Ventadorn* (1934); (c) cf. the references given in *ReMMA*, p. 215; (d) Bibl. Nat. *f.22543*, p. 62. ¶ Records: (c) *Fr. Col. DF103*; (d) *Decca 20158*.

19. TROUVÈRES. The songs of the trouvères of northern France show more clearly defined contours than those of the troubadours, in their rhythm as well as in their formal structure. Modal rhythm can be applied in most cases, usually without much ambiguity. Very likely there is a causal connection between the appearance of modal rhythm in the trouvère songs and its appearance at the same time and place in the polyphonic music of the School of Notre Dame at Paris (cf. Nos. 28ff). The great majority of the trouvère songs are written in one of three strictly fixed forms: the *ballade* (19a-c) with the scheme a a b (cf. the remark on the *canzo*, No. 18), the *rondeau* (19d, e) with the scheme A B a A a b A B (capital letters indicate the refrain, that is, repeated text), and the *virelai* (19f, g) with the scheme A b b a A. Example 19d shows a rondeau notated in two ways: first, running on continuously as it is sung; second, in the abbreviated arrangement commonly used in modern editions, with the figures 1 to 8 indicating the succession of the lines of the poem. No. 19f illustrates the corresponding method for the virelai. Less clearly defined and less frequent is the *rotrouenge* (h), the characteristic feature of which seems to be the repetition of the same melody for all the lines of a stanza except the last, or the last two: a a a a B or a a a b B. The *lai* (i) is an extended poem of a narrative or contemplative character, essentially different from the lyrical character of the other types. It was also known under the name *descort* (disorder), and this name is appropriate because of the irregularity of form as well as the intended obscurity of text encountered in this type. In our example the sections C, F, and G are omitted. See W. Apel, *Harvard Dictionary of Music* (1944), p. 392, for the complete structure. ¶ Sources: (a) J. B. Beck, *Le Chansonnier Cangé* (1927), i, 62ᵛ; (b) *ibid.*, i, 118ʳ; (c) F. Gennrich, *Rondeaux, Virelais und Balladen*, 1 (1921), 291; (d) *ibid.*, p. 85; (e) *ibid.*, p. 84; (f) *ibid.*, p. 37; (g) *ibid.*, p. 129; (h) F. Gennrich, *Die altfranzösische Rotrouenge* (1925), p. 40; (i) A. Jeanroy and P. Aubry, *Lais et descorts français* (1901), p. 87. ¶ Records: (a and b) *AS-18 (GSE*, pp. 377, 343); (e) *Lum-30058 (ReMMA*, p. 471).

20. MINNESINGERS. The German minnesinger movement (*Minne* = courtly love) originated around 1150, under the influence of the Provençal troubadours. Textual as well as musical considerations lead to a rhythmic rendition of their songs in even note values (4/4 meter). Indeed, the "weightiness" of this meter is more appropriate for the German songs than the "elegance" of modal rhythm which fits so well the melodies of the French trouvères. Example 20a is one of the few surviving twelfth-century minnesinger

melodies. Its somewhat irregular rhythm and free through-composed form indicate the influence of early troubadour style. Walther von der Vogelweide's celebrated Palestine Song (probably written in 1228) is an example of the most important form of minnesinger music, the *Bar*, with the scheme a a b, the German counterpart of the troubadour *canzo* (cf. No. 18) and the trouvère *ballade* (cf. No. 19). Owing to the large number of his songs extant, Neithart von Reuenthal stands out as the central figure of minnesinger music. His charming song "Der May" is particularly interesting for its use of successive thirds. ¶ Sources: (a) F. L. Saran, *Die Jenaer Liederhandschrift* (1902), 11, 20; (b) R. F. Molitor, in *Sammelbände der Internationalen Musikgesellschaft*, xii, 475, facs. (cf. also *AdHM*, 204); (c) *DTOe 37*. 1, 33; (d) *ibid.*, p. 32. ¶ Record: (b) *Decca 20158*.

21. LAUDE. The laude are Italian devotional hymns. They originated in the thirteenth century, probably in connection with the activity of St. Francis of Assisi (1182-1226), and until the nineteenth century they continued to play an important part in the religious life of the Italian people. Most of the medieval laude are written in the refrain form of the French virelai (cf. No. 19), freely modified. Example 21b is one of the few laude showing the strict form of the virelai, or, as it was called in Italy, *ballata* (cf. No. 51). A rendition in free rhythm seems preferable to the strictly metrical rendition used in Liuzzi's edition. (Cf. also No. 94.) ¶ Sources: (a) F. Liuzzi, *La Lauda . . .* (1935), 11, 30; (b) *ibid.*, 11, 375; (c) *ibid.*, 11, 259 (cf. also *AdHM*, p. 211). ¶ Records: (a) *AS-8 (GSE*, p. 555); (c) *Lum-32018 (ReMMA*, p. 472).

22. CANTIGAS. The cantigas are Spanish devotional hymns of the thirteenth century, mostly in honor of the Virgin Mary (Cantigas de Santa Maria). They were collected in various magnificent volumes for the king Alfonso el Sabio (1252-1284), who probably himself contributed part of the contents. Most of them are written in the refrain form of the French virelai (cf. No. 19), or, as the Spanish called it, *villancico*. Modifications of the strict virelai form occur, though less frequently than with the Italian laude (cf. No. 21). ¶ Sources: (a) J. Ribera, *La Musica de las Cantigas* (1922), no. 5; (b) *ibid.*, no. 4; (c) *ibid.*, no. 132.

23. ENGLISH SONGS. Among the few early English songs that survive, those ascribed to St. Godric are the most interesting. As in the case of other early monophonic songs, we prefer a free rhythmic rendition over one in modal rhythm (cf. *ReMMA*, p. 241). "Worldes blis" is a characteristic example of thirteenth-century Anglo-Saxon poetry, which has been described as "sad and foreboding" (cf. *ReMMA*, p. 242). ¶ Sources: cf. E. Trend, in *Music and Letters*, ix (1928), 112; (a) frontispiece in G. Saintsbury, *History of English Prosody*; (b) facsimile in H. E. Wooldridge, *Early English Harmony*, vol. 1 (1897), pl. 23.

24. MASTERSINGERS. The mastersingers (G. *Meistersinger*) were craftsmen who continued the tradition of the

minnesingers. They flourished particularly in the sixteenth century, with Hans Sachs as their most outstanding representative. Their main musical form is the *Bar* (cf. No. 20), consisting of "zween Stollen und ein Abgesang" (two opening strains and one concluding strain). This form and other technical procedures of the mastersinger school are aptly set forth in Richard Wagner's *Die Meistersinger* (Act I, 3, and III, 2). ¶Source: G. Münzer, *Das Singebuch des Adolf Puschmann* (1907), p. 79.

25. PARALLEL ORGANUM. Organum is the collective name for the various methods of early polyphony, from about 800 to about 1200. The present examples illustrate the earliest type of organum, characterized by the use of two voices in parallel fifths and fourths. The original melody, borrowed from Gregorian chant and designated as *vox principalis*, lies above the added voice part, known as *vox organalis*. The first four examples (a, 1–3; b, 1) illustrate the strictly parallel organum, which also existed in three- and four-voice modifications (composite organum) resulting from octave duplications. The fifth (b, 2) shows a freer type, in which the two voice parts start and end in unison. The last example (c), from the Orkneys, illustrates the use of parallel thirds, which was restricted to the British Isles and Scandinavia (cf. *ReMMA*, p. 388f). ¶Sources: (a) M. Gerbert, *Scriptores ecclesiastici . . .* , 3 vols. (1784; facsimile ed., 1931), I, 167; (b) *ibid.*, p. 185ff; (c) cf. *AdHM*, p. 167.

26. FREE ORGANUM. About the year 1000 the parallel organum was replaced by one using mainly contrary motion of the two voice parts. The vox principalis (or *cantus firmus*, as it may be called) is now usually the lower part. No. 26a is based on the Kyrie-trope "Cunctipotens [or Omnipotens] genitor" (cf. No. 15b), while No. 26c uses the Alleluia "Angelus Domini" (cf. No. 13) as a cantus firmus. The latter composition (26c), which comes from the School of Chartres in Northern France, is remarkable for the use of extended melismas (note against note) in both voice parts. It also illustrates a characteristic manner of performance, traces of which survived as late as the sixteenth century (cf. No. 127), namely, the alternate use of the entire choir and a few picked soloists, the former for the monophonic, the latter for the polyphonic sections. The origin of this procedure is found in the fact that the same principle of alternation occurs in all the Gregorian graduals, alleluias, responsoria, etc. (see Nos. 12, 13), and that only the solo sections (that is, the verses) of the chants were composed polyphonically, for a few solo singers of special ability and training, probably not more than two or three for each part. It was not until the middle of the sixteenth century that larger choirs were used for the performance of polyphonic church music (motets, masses, etc.). ¶Sources: (a) Treatise *Ad organum faciendum* (cf. *ReMMA*, p. 262), and *Oxford History of Music*, I (2nd ed., 1929), 45; (b) *ApNPM*, pp. 205, 207; (c) *AdHM*, p. 175. ¶Records: (c) *Victor-13555* and *VM-739*.

27. MELISMATIC ORGANUM. In the twelfth century yet another type of organum evolved, characterized by the use of extended melismas in the upper part against fewer, sustained notes in the cantus firmus. This important innovation was cultivated in the School of St. Martial at Limoges in Southern France and in the School of Santiago de Compostela in Galicia. Example 27a uses as a cantus firmus an extended trope of the Christmas gradual "Viderunt omnes" (cf. *LU*, p. 409). While this composition shows the technique of a "melismatic" upper part only in spots, the example from Compostela (b) is entirely based on this technique. (For its cantus firmus, cf. Nos. 15 and 26a.) ¶Sources: (a) *ApNPM*, p. 209 (cf. also the differing transcription in *AdHM*, p. 179); (b) H. Anglès, *El Codex musical de Las Huelgas* (1938), III, 1.

28. BENEDICAMUS DOMINO. The *Benedicamus Domino, Deo gratias* is a salutation of the Roman liturgy which is sung at the end of all offices, to various melodies (*toni*). The first of these melodies was very frequently used as a tenor for polyphonic compositions throughout the twelfth and thirteenth centuries. The compositions given here, all based on this melody, represent a survey of the development of polyphonic music during this period. Number 28a is the plainsong melody, sung responsorially: "Benedicamus Domino" by the soloist(s), "Deo gratias" by the choir. In conformity with the practice explained under No. 26, the first section only is usually composed polyphonically, the choral answer being in plainsong. Number 28b is a two-voice organum from the School of Compostela, similar in style to the "Cunctipotens genitor" (No. 27b). Number 28c illustrates the epochal innovation of the School of Notre Dame (Magister Leoninus, fl. *c.* 1175), that is, the introduction of a strictly measured rhythm, in one of the rhythmic modes. Number 28d is a *clausula*, that is, a polyphonic composition using not the entire chant (more properly, the entire soloist section of the chant), but only a single melismatic passage thereof, in the present case that for the word *Domino*. These clausulae, which form a large portion of the repertory of the School of Notre Dame, were used either as substitutes for the corresponding sections of full organa or (more likely) as independent compositions in connection with plainsong. Thus, in the present case, the word *Benedicamus* would be sung by the soloists in plainsong, the word *Domino* by the same soloists in two-voice composition, and the *Deo gratias* by the choir in plainsong. Number 28e is another clausula *Domino*, in which the plainsong melody is sung twice (double cursus), with a shift of the rhythmic pattern for the second statement. Numbers 28f through 28i illustrate various stages of the development of the thirteenth-century motet, a type which may be described as a clausula in which a full text is provided for each of the upper parts. In fact, the motet was originated through exactly this process of textual addition, as can be seen from No. 28h. Another illustration of this process is given in the next example (28i), showing a clausula, "Flos Filius," with two derivative motets. The tenor of these compositions is taken from the re-

sponsorium "Stirps Jesse" (In Nativitatem B. M. V.), but its melody is the same as that of "Benedicamus Domino." Another point of interest presented by the motet III of this group is the use of the refrain *C'est la fin* (at the end of the French text) which is taken—text as well as music—from the trouvère song "Vos n'aler" (No. 19f). For another example illustrating this practice of incorporating popular refrains into motets (refrain motet) see No. 32d. ¶ Sources: (a) *LU*, p. 124; (b) H. Anglès, *El Codex musical de Las Huelgas* (1938), III, 47; (c) Codex Florence, Bibl. Laur. *plut. 29, 1* (*F*), fols. 86v, 87r; (d) *ibid.*, fol. 88v; (e) *ibid.*, fol. 88v; (f) Codex Wolfenbüttel *1206* (*W₂*), fol. 179v; (g) P. Aubry, *Cent motets du XIIIe siècle* (1908), Codex Bamberg *Ed. IV. 6* (*Ba*), No. 31; (h) Y. Rokseth, *Polyphonies du XIII siècle* (1936–39); Codex Montpellier, Fac. des Méd. *H 196* (*Mo*), No. 143; (i) *ApNPM*, pp. 237, 273, 285.

29. ORGANUM "HEC DIES" IN LEONINUS' STYLE. This composition provides a fuller illustration of the technique of Leoninus, a first example of which is given in No. 28c. The source of this extended composition is the Easter gradual "Haec dies" (cf. No. 12). In conformity with the principles explained under No. 26, only the solo sections of this chant are composed polyphonically, the others being sung by the choir in plainsong. It will be noticed that there is a striking contrast between the free and irregular style of the sections *Hec dies* and *Confitemini* on the one side, and the strictly contrapuntal style of the sections *Domino, Quoniam, In seculum,* on the other. The current designation for these is organal style and discant style. The sections in discant style are clausulae, which appear here as parts of an organum. This was doubtless their original status, whereas subsequently they were taken out of their contexts and became independent pieces in their own right. A comparison of our rendition with the widely differing transcription given in *AdHM*, p. 217, will show the considerable uncertainty which still prevails in the problems offered by the music of this period. ¶ Source: Codex Wolfenbüttel *677* (*W₁*), fol. 27. ¶ Records: *Victor-13555; GSE*, p. 258 (both after *AdHM*).

30. CLAUSULAE FOR "HEC DIES." As previously explained (No. 28d), a clausula is a polyphonic composition of a short passage of a chant. From a study of the gradual "Haec dies" (see No. 12) it will be seen that the clausulae of the present example (see also No. 29) are based on melismatic passages of the chant, that is, on passages in which a florid melody consisting of numerous notes occurs with a single word or a single syllable. In fact, all the clausulae are invariably based on such "melismas," never on the syllabic sections of the chant. The clausulae of the present example are written in the style of Magister Perotinus (*c.* 1160–1220), the successor of Leoninus. A comparison with the corresponding sections of Leoninus' organum (No. 29) illustrates the general tendency of Perotinus towards a more crystallized and more concise style of composition. It should be noted that the present example is not a unified composition in the proper sense of the word. It merely shows a number of

clausulae as they may have been used in connection with plainsong. ¶ Source: *W₁*, fols. 46v–48v.

31. ORGANUM "HEC DIES" IN PEROTINUS' STYLE. The tendency pointed out in No. 30 appears again in the present composition. Perotinus also took the step from two-voice composition to composition in three and four parts. Our example shows somewhat less than half of the complete organum, to the word "bonus." ¶ Source: *W₁*, fol. 81.

32. MOTETS FOR "HEC DIES." Regarding the origin of the motet, see the explanations given under No. 28f-i. It goes without saying that, after the introduction of the motet as a textual derivative of clausulae, motets were also composed independently, that is to say, without the use of a pre-existing clausula. The examples of the present group illustrate various special methods of motet composition. In the first (a), the original melody for the words *Hec dies* is enlarged through repetition, according to the scheme a a b a, a scheme which is somewhat similar to that of the medieval rondeau (see No. 19d, e). The second example (b) shows the substitution of a French for a Latin text in the upper part, a method which is frequently encountered in the thirteenth-century repertory of motets. No. 32c is an example of the so-called *conductus motet,* that is, one in which the upper parts show identical text as well as identical rhythm, as is the case with the polyphonic conductus (see Nos. 38, 39). There is reason to believe that this was one of the earliest types, if not the earliest type, of motet. This also shows an interesting stylistic feature of thirteenth-century composition, the so-called exchange of parts (G. *Stimmtausch;* see the section "Se conformans"). It illustrates an extremely dissonant style which is not infrequent in music of the early thirteenth century. The tenor and middle part (duplum) form a pair of consonant voices, as do the middle part and upper part (triplum), whereas the combination of all three parts produces sharp dissonances. (Cf. *ApNPM,* p. 280.) The fourth motet (d) is another example of the refrain motet which is explained under No. 28i. (For the refrain see No. 19d.) The last composition of this group (e) is an "instrumental motet," if this somewhat self-contradictory term be permitted; that is, an instrumental composition written in the style of a motet. Several such compositions, to be performed on viols (one of them is called "In Seculum viellatoris"), exist in the Codex Bamberg. A particularly interesting feature of this composition is the extensive use of hocket. This means the truncation of a melodic line into short fragments (frequently single notes) which are given to two voices in quick alternation. ¶ Sources: (a) *Mo*, No. 184; (b) *Mo*, no. 45 and *Ba*, no. 96; (c) *W₂*, fols. 126–7; (d) *Mo*, no. 85; (e) *Ba*, no. 108.

33. TWO MOTETS. These two compositions illustrate the development of music around and after 1250, at the time of Franco of Cologne. The triplum (that is, the highest voice) now becomes the predominant part, melodically as well as

rhythmically. In the first example (a) exchange of parts is extensively used (see No. 32c). Another interesting feature is the extended vocalizations on the syllable "a—." It should be noticed that vocalization is required for all the textless parts of early polyphonic music, particularly for the tenors of all the organa, clausulae, and motets. (Instrumental performance of these parts, frequently suggested in modern writings, is extremely unlikely.) The second motet (b) illustrates the complete breaking away of the motet from its liturgical connection. The tenor no longer is a Gregorian cantus firmus, but a freely invented melodic phrase repeated several times in the character of a *basso ostinato*. All the texts are comments on the gay life of Paris; the tenor apparently reproduces a familiar street cry. ¶ Sources: (a) *Mo*, no. 339; (b) *Mo*, no. 319. ¶ Record: (a) *Lum-32027* (*ReMMA*, p. 474).

34. PETRUS DE CRUCE: Motet. Petrus de Cruce, who lived in the second half of the thirteenth century, made an important contribution towards the development of musical rhythm by introducing quick note values (semibreves) to be sung—in groups up to seven—in the place of a quarternote (brevis). There results a somewhat mannered style in which quick parlando passages alternate with relatively long notes. A complete disregard of what are considered today the most elementary principles of textual declamation is a typical by-product of this style. ¶ Source: *Mo*, no. 254.

35. MOTET "JE CUIDOIE." Judging from its style, this motet also may well be a composition of Petrus de Cruce's. It makes ample use of the hocket technique explained under No. 32. ¶ Source: *Mo*, no. 332.

36. ADAM DE LA HALLE. Adam de la Halle (*c.* 1230–1287) holds an interesting historical position on the border line between an old and a new school of thought. He was one of the last to cultivate the monophonic songs of the trouvère period, and one of the first to transfer them to the field of polyphonic music, thus inaugurating a trend which predominated in the French *Ars nova* of the fourteenth century. In his style he is rather conservative, except for a more liberal use of ornamenting figures than was customary before him. Number 36a is a monophonic ballade; 36b is a three-voice rondeau; while 36c is interesting as an early instance of the modern rondo, a b a b a, a form which did not come into general use until after 1650 (see No. 147). ¶ Source: E. de Coussemaker, *Oeuvres complètes du trouvère Adam de la Halle* (1872), pp. 35, 230, 232. ¶ Record: (c) *GSE*, p. 2.

37. TWO–VOICE TROPE: "Rex virginum." This composition is an example of a special type of thirteenth-century music which is thought to be of British origin (according to J. Handschin; cf. *ReMMA*, p. 393ff). The main characteristics of these "insular" compositions (mostly preserved in fascicle 11 of *W₁*) are the use of (1) a non-Gregorian tenor;

(2) a prevailingly syllabic style; (3) note-against-note technique for all the parts; (4) identical text for both parts. It may be noticed that all these traits are found in the earliest organa of the ninth through the eleventh centuries (see Nos. 25, 26). In regard to the first of these four characteristics, it may be said that our example, like the eleventh-century "Cunctipotens genitor" (No. 26a), is based on a Kyrie-trope (Kyrie, *Rex virginum* . . .). Moreover, both tropes use the same melody, that of the Kyrie of the Mass IV (see No. 15). The other three traits occur also in the thirteenth-century conductus (see Nos. 38, 39). ¶ Source: *W₁*, fol. 176r.

38. CONDUCTUS: "Roma gaudens jubila." As explained under No. 17, the Latin lyric poetry of the twelfth and thirteenth centuries was generically designated as conductus. In the thirteenth century these songs were composed polyphonically, mostly in three parts, and it is to this type of music that the term conductus usually applies. The general style of conductus composition is the same as that described under No. 37, except that the tenor, instead of being borrowed from the liturgical repertory, is freely invented, text as well as melody. The conductus, therefore, represents the earliest type of completely free polyphonic composition. Our transcription may be compared with that in *ReMMA*, p. 309. Regarding the question as to whether the conductus should be rendered in even note values or in alternating longs and shorts (modal rhythm), cf. *ApNPM*, p. 224. ¶ Source: *W₁*, fol. 107r.

39. CONDUCTUS: "Hac in anni janua." Compositions like this one lend themselves well to a study of thirteenth-century three-voice harmony (or counterpoint). The use of full triads—that is, of triads including the third—and of sharply dissonant "appoggiaturas" may be noticed. ¶ Source: *W₁*, fol. 71r (cf. also *ApNPM*, p. 221).

40. MONOPHONIC DANCES. All the dances of the thirteenth and fourteenth centuries belong to one main type, known as *estampie*. The estampie, an early example of which was encountered in the "Kalenda maya" of No. 18d, is characterized by a form similar to that of the sequences from which it is doubtless derived. It consists of four to seven sections, called *punctus*, each of which is repeated, with a different ending for the repetition. In some cases the same two endings are used for all the sections, as, for instance, in our first two examples here given (a, b), a type for which the term "rounded estampie" may be suggested. If the dance had only three or four puncti, it was also known under the name of *ductia*. ¶ Sources: (a) P. Aubry, *Estampies et danses royales* (1906), p. 14; (b) *ibid.*, p. 19; (c) J. Wolf, in *Archiv für Musikwissenschaft*, I, 22 (facsimile in J. Stainer, *Early Bodleian Music*, vol. I, pl. VII). ¶ Record: *AS-16* (*GSE*, p. 555) contains, first side, No. 40c (repetitions of punctus 1–3 are omitted), No. 40a (drum accompaniment added), No. 41a; second side, No. 40b (abbreviated performance; only the sections 1a, 1b, 2a, 3b, 4a, 5b, 6a, 7b are played), No. 59a.

41. TWO-VOICE DANCES. Both examples are polyphonic elaborations of the type described above (No. 40) as ductia. No. 41a has the basic ductia melody in the lower part. It consists of three short sections (1, 2, 3), each of which is repeated with a different ending (1a, 1b . . .). The whole melody is stated twice, each time with a different counterpoint in the upper part (4, 5, 6). No. 41b is based on a ductia melody of two puncti (1, 2) which are subsequently transferred to the upper part (3, 4) and transposed to the upper fifth. ¶ Sources: (a) J. Wolf, *Handbuch der Notationskunde* (1910), p. 224; (b) *ApNPM*, p. 247. ¶ Record: (a) See under No. 40.

42. "SUMER IS ICUMEN IN." This composition is too well known to require explanatory remarks. Suffice it to say that, according to recent investigations, its date is probably about seventy years later than has been assumed (cf. M. F. Bukofzer, *Sumer is icumen in*, 1944). ¶ Source: British Museum, *Harleian 978*. ¶ Record: *Columbia-5715*.

43. ROMAN DE FAUVEL: "Detractor est." The *Roman de Fauvel* is an important literary and musical source of the early fourteenth century, containing monophonic songs and motets inserted in a continuous narrative. The motets are written in the style of Petrus de Cruce (see Nos. 34 and 35), but some of them show features characteristic of fourteenth-century music. Notable among these is the isorhythmic structure of the tenor. This means that the melody of the tenor is organized rhythmically on the basis of a rather elaborate pattern of note values which is repeated throughout the entire tenor. In the present motet this pattern (the so-called *talea*) comprises six measures. The principle of isorhythmic construction is but an amplification and elaboration of the shorter rhythmic patterns usually found in the tenors of thirteenth-century motets (e.g., Nos. 32b, c). Nevertheless, the isorhythmic technique presented a novel procedure, since it meant abandoning the rhythmic modes which governed the rhythmic structure of nearly all the tenors in the music of the thirteenth century. ¶ Source: Joh. Wolf, *Geschichte der Mensuralnotation* (1904), vol. II, no. 6 (our transcription differs in many details from the one given in Wolf's vol. III).

44. GUILLAUME DE MACHAUT: "S'il estoit nulz." Machaut is the outstanding representative of French fourteenth-century music. His compositions embody the great achievements of the *Ars nova*, achievements which lie in the direction of liberation, secularization, refinement, expressiveness and, one may even say, Romanticism. Machaut's motets are the most conservative of his compositions, being evolved from the motet of the thirteenth century, but even in these works the novelty of style is striking, particularly as regards suppleness of rhythm and of melodic design. The present motet is isorhythmic (see No. 43), with a talea comprising five 3/2 measures; the fourth talea is shortened. As usual in Machaut's motets, the present example has a double cursus, that is, the plainsong melody (designated in this connection

as *color*) is stated twice. The second statement (B) has nearly the same structure as the first, but the notes are shifted to other positions, a procedure which originated in thirteenth-century clausulae such as No. 28e. ¶ Source: F. Ludwig, *Guillaume de Machaut, Musikalische Werke*, III, 25.

45. GUILLAUME DE MACHAUT: "Je puis trop bien." With Machaut begins the long line of composers, extending throughout the fourteenth and fifteenth centuries, who cultivated the trouvère ballade (see No. 19a-c) as an elaborate form of polyphonic music. The freedom, subtlety, and expressiveness of melody, as well as the variety of rhythm, are in marked contrast to the rigidly patterned style of the thirteenth century. This contrast, no doubt, marks the beginning of a new art, an *Ars nova* in the true sense of the word. ¶ Source: F. Ludwig, *Guillaume de Machaut, Musikalische Werke*, I, 31. ¶ Record: *AS-67* (*GSE*, p. 274).

46. GUILLAUME DE MACHAUT: Two virelais. Machaut wrote monophonic as well as polyphonic virelais. His monophonic "Comment qu'a moy" is a most charming song, written in a folk-like style which is astonishingly similar to the style of present-day French folksong. No less admirable is the artistic refinement of the polyphonic "Plus dure," an exquisite masterpiece of musical art. ¶ Source: F. Ludwig, *Guillaume de Machaut, Musikalische Werke*, I, 72, 86.

47. JACOPIN SELESSES. This composition has been selected in order to represent one of the least-explored periods of music history, the late fourteenth century. Very few compositions of this period are available for study because of the extraordinary difficulties presented by their notation. The most striking characteristic of these compositions is their rhythmic complexity, which indeed has never been paralleled in all music history. ¶ Source: *ApNPM*, p. 423.

48. BAUDE CORDIER. Baude Cordier represents the transition between the mannerism of the late fourteenth century (see No. 47) and the new classicism of the fifteenth century, embodied by Dufay and Binchois (see Nos. 65ff). His "Amans ames" follows the tradition of the past, while his "Belle bonne" is remarkably progressive, particularly because of its use of imitation for the beginning. This composition, a New Year's present to the poet's ladylove, was ingeniously written in the shape of a heart, a charming symbol of the idea of the poem, and perhaps also a pun on the composer's name. ¶ Source: *ApNPM*, pp. 175, 427.

49. JACOPO DA BOLOGNA. Numbers 49 to 54 serve to illustrate the Italian *Ars nova*, a movement of no less artistic significance than the contemporary movement in France. During the first half of the fourteenth century, two-part writing was commonly employed, with the upper part forming a florid counterpoint to the longer notes of the lower part. The preferred form of this period was the madrigal, which, as a poetic form, consists of two or three strophes of

three lines each, followed by a final strophe (*ritornello*) of two lines. The musical form follows closely that of the poetry, the same music (a) being used for the two (or three) stanzas, and different music (b) for the ritornello, so that the form a a b (or a a a b) results. ¶ Source: *Codex Reina* (Paris, Bibl. Nat., *fonds fr. nouv. acq. 6771*), fol. 3v. ¶ Record: *GSE*, p. 240.

50. GIOVANNI DA FLORENTIA: "Nel mezzo." This is an example of the eleven-line madrigal, with the modified scheme a a a b b. ¶ Source: Joh. Wolf, *Geschichte der Mensuralnotation* (1904), vols. II, III, no. 38.

51. GIOVANNI DA FLORENTIA: "Io son un pellegrin." This is an example of the Italian ballata, a form which is identical with (and evidently taken over from) the French virelai, A b b a A (cf. Nos. 19 and 46, also 21 and 22). ¶ Source: Paris, Bibl. Nat., *fonds ital. 568*, fol. 42v. ¶ Record: *AS-8 (GSE*, p. 555).

52. GHIRARDELLO DA FIRENZE. A particularly interesting form belonging to the early Italian *Ars nova* is the *caccia* (chase, hunt). Its literary subjects are hunting or fishing scenes full of lively description. The musical form is a strict canon in two parts at the distance of eight or more measures, which is usually supported by a free (i.e., not imitating) tenor in longer note values. ¶ Source: W. Th. Marrocco, *14th-Century Italian Cacce* (1942), p. 70. ¶ Record: *AS-59 (GSE*, p. 557).

53. FRANCESCO LANDINI: "Amor c'al tuo suggetto." Landini is the outstanding master of the late Italian *Ars nova,* during the second half of the fourteenth century. His compositions are usually in three parts, not in two as was customary before him. His preferred form is the ballata, derived from the French virelai, while the earlier Italian masters cultivated chiefly the indigenous madrigal. Stylistically, his most conspicuous achievement over his predecessors is the much greater subtlety and variety of the polyphonic texture, particularly in its rhythmic aspect. For this he is evidently indebted to Machaut, whom, however, he surpasses in the sweetness and expressiveness of his melodies. ¶ Source: F. Ellinwood, *The Works of Francesco Landini* (1939), no. 103.

54. FRANCESCO LANDINI: "Sy dolce non sono." This composition affords one of the few examples to be found in medieval music of a deviation from the standard forms which were traditionally used for the musical structure of a composition based on a poetic text. Although the poem is an eleven-line madrigal, it is not set to music in the corresponding musical form, a a a b (see No. 49), but is through-composed. Thus it anticipates the procedure which was universally adopted for the sixteenth-century madrigal. On the other hand, its connection with the tradition of the fourteenth century appears from the fact that it has an isorhythmic tenor, with a talea of seven measures. ¶ Source: F. Ellinwood, *The Works of Francesco Landini* (1939), facsimile facing p. 34.

55. JOHANNES CICONIA: "Et in terra pax." While the "proto-renaissance" of the fourteenth century had led to a striking superiority of secular over sacred music, the pendulum began to swing back with the advent of the fifteenth century. The first indication of this reversal is to be found in the numerous compositions of single items of the Ordinary of the Mass (Kyrie, Gloria, Credo, Sanctus, and Agnus Dei) which preceded the composition of complete Masses (see No. 66). Ciconia's "Et in terra pax" is a Gloria, the initial phrase ("Gloria in excelsis Deo") being sung in plainsong. It shows characteristic tendencies toward clarity and simplicity, toward a polyphonic texture with greater participation of the lower parts (which are probably instrumental), and toward dignified expression. A peculiarity of this composition is the use of the same music for two sections of the Gloria text, from "Laudamus te" to "filius Patris" and from "Qui tollis" to "Dei Patris." ¶ Source: Ch. van den Borren, *Polyphonia sacra* (1932), p. 88.

56. GUILLAUME LEGRANT. Legrant's Credo is another example of the church music of the early fifteenth century. It is interesting for its alternation of sections in two and in three parts, the former probably for soloists, the latter for the choir (see also No. 64). The choral sections are in full chordal style (familiar style) and provide a most interesting insight into the harmonic idiom of the period. ¶ Source: Same as No. 55, p. 127.

57. SCHOOL OF WORCESTER. To judge from the scarce remnants of fourteenth-century English music, the School of Worcester played a leading role in its development. The examples given here illustrate the strong hold which the tradition of the thirteenth century retained in England at a time when France and Italy had made decisive steps in entirely new directions. They show the influence of the conductus style, which continued in English music well into the fifteenth century. A particularly obvious indication of thirteenth-century style is the *Stimmtausch* (exchange of parts) between the two upper voices in the "Alleluia psallat" (e.g., measures 2 and 6). The Gloria (57b) is interesting mostly as an example of the sixth-chord style, usually called fauxbourdon, which is frequently encountered in the English sources of the period and which differs in the position of the cantus firmus from the true fauxbourdon of French fifteenth-century music, as exemplified by Dufay. The English type has the cantus firmus in the tenor, the French in the soprano. ¶ Source: A. Hughes, *Worcester Mediaeval Harmony* (1928), pp. 83, 39. ¶ Record: (a) *Victor-13559* and *VM-739*.

58. ORGAN ESTAMPIE. The main interest of the present example lies in the fact that it represents the earliest keyboard music which has been preserved. It occurs, together with a few other pieces, in the so-called Robertsbridge Codex of about 1325 (cf. *ApNPM,* p. 37f). It is a long composition in the form of the estampie (see No. 40), but far removed from the original dance connotation of this form. Three of six puncti are reproduced here. From the stylistic point of

view, the old-fashioned parallel fifths and the hocket passages are noteworthy. Although this composition is usually considered to be of English origin, internal features, particularly notational details, point to Italy. ¶ Source: H. E. Wooldridge, *Early English Harmony,* vol. 1 (1897), plate 43.

59. ITALIAN DANCES. A considerable number of monophonic Italian dance melodies, evidently written for the vielle (viola) are preserved in a fourteenth-century manuscript in the British Museum. They all are written in the form of the estampie, most of them extremely long. Two of the shorter examples are reproduced here. The "Lamento di Tristan" is certainly one of the most charming compositions in the entire literature for stringed instruments. It is particularly interesting for its unmistakable folk-like flavor. The main dance is followed by a *Nachtanz* (La Rotta) in different meter. This composition as well as the Saltarello belongs to the type of "rounded estampie" (see No. 40). In both examples the prima volta closes on the supertonic of the secunda volta. ¶ Source: Brit. Mus. *Add. 29987,* fol. 63r–63v. ¶ Record: (a) *AS-16* (*GSE,* p. 555).

60. OSWALD VON WOLKENSTEIN. During the fourteenth century, Germany made a late and slow start in the field of polyphonic music. Wolkenstein is the first composer in this development from whose work a considerable number of compositions have been preserved. In these, the influence of the minnesinger tradition combines with that of the French *Ars nova.* The latter influence is particularly patent in Wolkenstein's "Der May," which is an adaptation of a composition by the French fourteenth-century composer J. Vaillant. But under Wolkenstein's hands the composition has gained rather than lost in charm and freshness. It is one of the earliest known examples of word painting, and one which, in spite of its primitiveness, surpasses many later attempts in the same direction. A comparison with Janequin's program chanson *L'Alouette* (No. 107) is interesting in this respect. ¶ Source: *DTOe* IX. 1, 179.

61. JOHN DUNSTABLE: "O rosa bella." The history of English music is striking for its irregular and eruptive line of evolution, involving, as it does, short periods of extraordinary flowering between centuries of slow progress or almost complete stagnation. As has been pointed out previously (see No. 57), English music during the fourteenth century hardly moved beyond the limits of thirteenth-century style and technique. This situation changed completely with John Dunstable, a composer of the highest significance who had a penetrating influence upon the further development of music, particularly in France (Dufay, Binchois), where he is believed to have spent a good deal of his life. He became the founder of what is known as the "Continental" school of fifteenth-century English music (Lionel Power, Bedingham, and others), in contrast to the "domestic" school (Cooke, Damett, Sturgeon), which largely retained the conservative methods of the fourteenth century. Dunstable's compositions are admirable mainly for the beauty of their melodic lines, in

the upper part as well as in the contrapuntal parts. They constitute a culmination of contrapuntal technique of no less significance than those represented by Josquin, Palestrina, and Bach. ¶ Source: *DTOe* VII, 229 (corrected after facs. IV).

62. JOHN DUNSTABLE: "Sancta Maria." The fifteenth-century return to church ideals not only led to an extensive activity in the field of Mass composition (see Nos. 55, 56), but also to a new interest in, and attitude toward, the motet. As early as the middle of the thirteenth century this form had been diverted from its original sacred affiliation by the intrusion of secular texts in the vernacular, a procedure which persisted throughout the fourteenth century (see No. 44). Dunstable was one of the first to cultivate the motet again in a style proper to its church use. He abandoned the poly-textuality as well as the cantus-firmus tenor of the medieval motet, and established the motet as a free composition on a liturgical text. Dunstable's "Sancta Maria" illustrates a particularly important trait of the composer's musical style, that is, the triadic construction of his melodies. For instance, the initial passage of the soprano part shows an unmistakable emphasis on the tones of the C-major triad at its beginning, followed by modulation into G major. The importance of this innovation can hardly be overestimated. Here we find the roots of that trend which led to the establishment of the triad as the cornerstone of musical technique. Another characteristic trait of Dunstable's style may be observed in the use of the upper appogiaturas which add so much to the eloquent expressiveness of the melodic lines. ¶ Source: *DTOe* VII, 197.

63. LIONEL POWER. This Sanctus is interesting as an illustration of the early experiments in four-voice harmony. Full triads in four voices, such as appear repeatedly here, are extremely scarce in music prior to this time. It was not until the establishment of the Flemish School under Ockeghem and Obrecht (see Nos. 73 to 78) that four-voice counterpoint became firmly established as the normal procedure. In this composition the plainsong Sanctus from the Mass XVII (for the Sundays of Advent and Lent; cf. *LU,* p. 61) is used as a cantus firmus in the tenor. The contratenor has no text in the original. The other three voices have the text syllables simultaneously, except for minor variants which are indicated in the score. ¶ Source: *The Old Hall MS* (new edition by A. Ramsbotham and H. B. Collins, 1935–38), III, 76.

64. DAMETT. As was pointed out under No. 61, Damett belongs to the "domestic" school of English music. It should be noticed, however, that the present example shows the influence of "Continental" thought to a larger extent than do other works of his and of his colleagues. For a discussion of the alternation of two-voice polyphonic sections for soloists and three-voice chordal sections for chorus (the chorus starts once more with the words "Ora pro nobis"), see No. 56. It may be noticed that our composition, although based on a liturgical text (antiphon for the Presentation of the Blessed

Virgin Mary; cf. *LU*, p. 1754) does not use the plainsong melody of this text. Thus it represents one of the early examples of free composition on a liturgical text. ¶ Source: Same as No. 63, vol. 1, p. 164. ¶ Record: *GSE*, p. 124.

65. GUILLAUME DUFAY: "Alma redemptoris mater." Dufay, together with Binchois, is the founder of the Burgundian School (formerly termed "First Netherlands School") which grew up in the splendid cultural sphere of the kingdom of Burgundy, under Philip the Good (1419–67) and Charles the Bold (1467–77). The music of the Burgundian School represents a reaction against the complexity and mannerism of the late *Ars nova*. Preceded by composers like Baude Cordier and strongly influenced by Dunstable, Dufay and Binchois developed a musical language whose beauty and tender sweetness are just as lively today as they were five hundred years ago. Dufay's "Alma redemptoris mater" belongs to a special type of cantus-firmus composition which may be termed discant motet. This means that the plainsong melody (cf. *LU*, p. 273) is used, not in the tenor as usual, but in the soprano (discant). While most of the tenor cantus firmi rigidly adhere to the original plainsong melody as well as to a strict rhythmical pattern (either isorhythmic or, later on, in evenly sustained notes; cf. No. 100), the discant cantus firmi are noticeable for their free treatment of the borrowed chant, melodically as well as rhythmically. Our example affords a clear insight into this technique by which a plainchant is changed ("secularized," one might almost say) into a graceful melody of an entirely different character. ¶ Source: *DTOe* xxvii.1, p. 19. ¶ Record: *AS-35* (*GSE*, p. 147).

66. GUILLAUME DUFAY: *Missa L'Homme armé.* Easily the most famous of all cantus firmi used for Mass compositions is the melody of a fifteenth-century French folksong, "L'Homme armé" (The armed man). It was used by numerous composers of Masses, throughout the fifteenth, sixteenth, and, less frequently, seventeenth centuries. Dufay's *Missa L'Homme armé* is one of the earliest of its kind. The Kyrie I uses the first phrase of the melody. The Agnus Dei III offers an example of the "canonic riddles" frequently encountered in the Masses of the fifteenth and early sixteenth centuries. The inscription "Cancer eat plenus et redeat medius" ("Let the crab proceed full and return half") indicates that the cantus firmus is to be sung twice, first in full note values, then in halved values and in retrograde motion (this being indicated by the word "returns"). Since, however, the crab's normal motion is backwards, the "proceeding" section actually is retrograde, and the "returning" section, therefore, in normal motion. The sign § in the first measure of line 5, p. 72, indicates the beginning of the second statement of the tune. The original notation of the Kyrie and the Agnus Dei is with a B-flat in the three lower parts only. ¶ Source: Cappella Sistina, *Cod. 49.*

67. GUILLAUME DUFAY: "Mon chier amy." This example is one of the numerous secular compositions of the Burgundian master. The prominent position which the bal-

lade had held during the fourteenth century (see Nos. 45, 47) somewhat declined during the fifteenth century. Nevertheless, Dufay and others continued to use this form as a vehicle of elaborate polyphonic style. The florid passages at the end of the various sections as well as the somewhat complex cross rhythms characterize this composition as belonging to Dufay's earlier period. ¶ Source: Oxford, Bodleian Library, *Ms. Canonici misc. 213* (c. 1450), fol. 134v.

68. GUILLAUME DUFAY: "Adieu m'amour." This composition, a rondeau, is a most beautiful example of Dufay's late style, characterized by translucent clarity of texture and subtle sensuousness of expression, as well as by the more consistent use of imitation. For the complete text see M. Loepelmann, *Die Liederhandschrift des Cardinals Rohan* (1923), no. 372. ¶ Source: F. Blume, *Das Chorwerk*, Heft 19, p. 22. ¶ Record: *AS-43* (*GSE*, p. 556).

69. GILLES BINCHOIS: "De plus en plus." The work of Binchois, the other great master of the Burgundian School, is not yet sufficiently known to permit an exact evaluation. It would seem that he tended towards a slightly more "popular" style, without, however, sacrificing the high artistic standards of Dufay. The beginning of the charming "De plus en plus" offers another example of the triadic type of melody which had been inaugurated by Dunstable (see No. 62). ¶ Source: F. Blume, *Das Chorwerk*, Heft 22, no. 5. ¶ Record: *AS-39* (*GSE*, p. 62).

70. GILLES BINCHOIS: "Files à marier." This delightful miniature composition is remarkable for its progressive character. It anticipates much of the joyful liveliness of the program chansons by Janequin (see No. 107), which, however, it far excels in true musical vitality. ¶ Source: J. Marix, *Les Musiciens de la cour de Bourgogne au XVe siècle* (1937), p. 46.

71. ARNOLD DE LANTINS. Arnold de Lantins is another member of the Burgundian School, probably a slightly older contemporary of Dufay and Binchois. At least some of his compositions fully come up to the artistic rank of the two leading masters. The triadic structure of the melody may be noticed. ¶ Source: Same as No. 67, fol. 52v. ¶ Record: *AS-39* (*GSE*, p. 556).

72. HUGO DE LANTINS. The compositions of this Burgundian master are remarkable for their frequent use of imitation. Since the more extended use of imitation normally belongs to a somewhat later period, Hugo de Lantins may be assumed to be a younger brother (or son?) of Arnold de Lantins. ¶ Source: *ApNPM*, p. 141.

73. JOHANNES OCKEGHEM: *Missa L'Homme armé.* With Ockeghem and his contemporary Obrecht a new and most important phase of music history begins, that is, the Flemish School (formerly called Second Netherlands School). In many respects the early Flemish music offers a sharp con-

trast to that of Burgundy. In the Burgundian School there was, by and large, an unmistakable emphasis on secular music, while both Ockeghem and Obrecht were active mainly in the field of church music. The Burgundian masters wrote numerous songs in which instruments participated, while the Flemish wrote chiefly masses and motets for a cappella chorus. Technically, one of their most important contributions was the final establishment of four-part writing as the normal texture of polyphonic music. This was accompanied by a clearer separation of the vocal ranges than had existed before. Finally, the ideal of a contrapuntal web consisting of four or more equally important parts was more clearly realized than before. The Kyrie of Ockeghem's *Missa L'Homme armé* uses the three phrases of the tune for its three sections, *Kyrie, Christe,* and *Kyrie.* The contrast between the figurate counterpoint of the two *Kyrie's* and the prevailingly chordal style of the *Christe* may be noticed. The Agnus Dei III offers a good example of the highly embroidered (figurate) counterpoint to be found in many compositions of Ockeghem's. ¶ Source: Complete Works, ed. by D. Plamenac, I, 99ff.

74. JOHANNES OCKEGHEM: "Ma maîtresse." In his secular compositions Ockeghem continued the tradition of Dufay. Distinctive features to be noticed in this example, a virelai, are the extended phrases and the individual character of the two accompanying parts, both of which are more figurate than the upper part. The contrasting meter and style of section B are also worth noticing. ¶ Source: Same as No. 73, p. 124. ¶ Record: *AS-1* (*GSE*, p. 554).

75. JOHANNES OCKEGHEM: "Ma bouche rit." This virelai is one of the most beautiful compositions of a master whose claims to recognition are often incorrectly based on feats of technical skill such as a 36-voice canon or a "Missa cuiusvis toni." A point of special interest is the continuous flow of the contrapuntal web, which never comes to a complete stop except at the end of each section. ¶ Source: *Odhecaton A* (edited by H. Hewitt, 1942), no. 54.

76. JACOB OBRECHT: "O beate Basili" and "O vos omnes." Although Ockeghem and Obrecht are usually named in one breath, the difference between their styles is no less considerable than in the case of other musical twins, such as Bach and Handel. Of the two, Obrecht is the more progressive, anticipating, as he does, a good many of the achievements of Josquin. His style is less embroidered, more structural and motival, than that of Ockeghem, and employs shorter phrases with more clearly marked cadences. More than anybody else, he deserves credit for the establishment of the technique of imitative counterpoint which became the foundation stone of sixteenth-century musical style. ¶ Source: Complete edition (by Joh. Wolf), Motetten, II, 85, and IV, 173.

77. JACOB OBRECHT: Kyrie and Agnus Dei. The two movements of the *Missa Sine Nomine* illustrate the "cyclical" treatment frequently found in masses of the Flemish era.

This means the use of the same motive for the beginning of all, or nearly all, the movements of the Mass. An interesting detail is the sequential passage near the end of the Agnus. ¶ Source: Complete edition (by Joh. Wolf), Missen, IV, 41.

78. JACOB OBRECHT: "Tsaat een meskin." Yet another of Obrecht's claims to eminence is based on his position in the history of instrumental music. He is the first composer to whom a considerable number of purely instrumental pieces is known to belong. His "Tsaat een meskin" ("A maiden sat"), obviously based on a Dutch folk tune, bears all the characteristic earmarks of the instrumental canzona (see Nos. 88, 118, 136, 175). The original melody is in the tenor. ¶ Source: Complete edition (by Joh. Wolf), Wereldlijke Werken XV/XVI, 7. ¶ Record: *AS-27* (*GSE*, p. 556).

79. LOYSET COMPÈRE: "Royne du ciel." Compère, a pupil of Ockeghem, is a member of the so-called School of Cambrai, which combined Flemish elements with the heritage of Dufay, who lived in Cambrai from 1450 till his death. Our example shows a mixture of progressive and archaic features. Among the former is the consistent use of imitation; among the latter, the use of a different text for the tenor, as in a thirteenth-century motet. The tenor repeats the phrase "Regina coeli" several times through ascending degrees of the scale, a method which may perhaps be explained as a sequential modification of an isorhythmic tenor. The complete composition is a rondeau, A B a a A a b A B, a strictly secular form which is used here with a religious text (for the full text see the source). ¶ Source: *Odhecaton A* (edited by H. Hewitt, 1942), no. 84.

80. HEINRICH FINCK. The rise of polyphonic music in Germany came very late, and it was not until the end of the fifteenth century, under Adam von Fulda, Heinrich Finck, and Alexander Agricola, that a continuous development started there, influenced, it would seem, by the figurate style of Ockeghem. The present composition skillfully combines the melodies of two Ambrosian hymns in the manner of a quodlibet, a form which was much in favor with the German composers of the fifteenth and sixteenth centuries (see No. 82). ¶ Source: *Das Chorwerk*, XXXII, 19.

81. CONRAD PAUMANN. Germany, though tardy in cultivating vocal polyphony, was ahead of the other nations in the field of organ music. Paumann's *Fundamentum organisandi* (1452) contains, in addition to numerous instructive examples of organ composition, a few organ pieces based on German folksongs. Some of these songs are preserved in a contemporary source of vocal music, the Lochamer Liederbuch. Our example shows one of these, "Mit ganczem Willen," in its original form (cf. the reconstruction by H. Rosenberg, in *ZMW*, XIV, 85), and in Paumann's beautiful organ composition. In the original manuscript the closing section of Paumann's composition is erroneously notated. Our rendition is based on the assumption that, beginning

with the a of the fifth measure from the end, the melody is written a third too high. ¶ Source: *Das Lochamer Liederbuch* (facsimile edition by K. Ameln, 1925), pp. 30, 72.

82, 83. GLOGAUER LIEDERBUCH. This interesting manuscript contains a considerable number of polyphonic compositions, vocal as well as instrumental. The quodlibet reproduced as No. 82 combines the melody of "O rosa bella" (see No. 61) with numerous snatches of German folksongs. A number of these occur separately in the Glogauer Liederbuch, and their beginnings are given here, together with the composition based on them, in order to make possible a study of the technique employed. The instrumental pieces contained in the Glogauer Liederbuch are among the earliest of their kind, aside from the "In seculum" compositions of the thirteenth century (see No. 32e). Particularly interesting are the various dances, for three or four instruments. The present example, "Der neue Bauernschwanz" (The new peasant dance) is especially remarkable for its *Nachtanz* (that is, second dance) in quick triple meter, the style of which comes surprisingly close to that of numerous "correntos" written before and after 1600 (*Fitzwilliam Virginal Book*, Frescobaldi). ¶ Source: *Das Glogauer Liederbuch,* new edition by H. Ringmann, vol. 1 (1936), pp. 40, 49, 87.

84. ORGAN PRELUDES. The numerous preludes contained in German sources from about 1450 to about 1520 constitute a tradition of particular interest, because they represent the earliest type of idiomatic keyboard music as distinct from types influenced by dance music (see No. 58) or vocal music (see No. 81b). The preludes contained in the tablature by Adam Ileborgh show a melodic line in rambling style and free rhythm, extending over a few sustained chords. Those from the Buxheim Organ Book usually alternate between free passages and sections in chordal style. The preludes of the early sixteenth century (tablatures by Leonhard Kleber and Johannes Kotter) show the tendency towards a more crystallized and concise style, melodically as well as harmonically and rhythmically. ¶ Sources: (a) and (b) W. Apel, "Die Tabulatur des Adam Ileborgh" (*ZMW*, xvi); (c) and (d) Buxheim Organ Book, *c.* 1470 (Munich, Staatsbibliothek, *Mus. Ms. 3725*), nos. 53 and 216; (e) and (f) Tablature of Leonhard Kleber, 1524 (Berlin, Staatsbibliothek, *Mus. Ms. Z. 26*), fols. 7v and 4v; (g) W. Apel, *Musik aus früher Zeit,* vol. 1.

85, 86. ENGLISH PART SONGS. Toward the end of the fifteenth century there appeared in England a modest flowering of secular music. Part songs of a more or less popular character (anachronistically designated in modern editions as "madrigals") were written by various composers, and even King Henry VII made some contributions to this repertory. The somewhat primitive style of the "Tappster, Drinker" suggests a slightly earlier date for this "bright and racy" drinking song (*c.* 1450) than for the rather nicely polished compositions given under No. 86. ¶ Sources: No. 85: John Stainer, *Early Bodleian Music,* ii (1901), 177; No. 86: Brit. Mus. *Add. 31922,* fols. 23v, 65v.

87. HEINRICH ISAAC: "Zwischen Berg und tiefem Tal." Heinrich Isaac is the first "international" composer of the Renaissance. Of Flemish extraction, he wrote German, Italian, and French songs as well as sacred and instrumental music. The present composition apparently is a polyphonic elaboration of a folksong which appears as a canon in the tenor and the bass, the other parts weaving around it in imitation and free figuration. ¶ Source: *DTOe* xiv.1, 26. ¶ Record: *AS-1* (*GSE*, p. 554).

88. HEINRICH ISAAC: Instrumental canzona. Among the various individual traits of Isaac's style the use of short, characteristic motives and the writing of extended sequential passages (see No. 77) are particularly striking. The present example illustrates both these traits as well as others indicative of that trend towards rationalization which characterizes the transition from the late Middle Ages to the early Renaissance. ¶ Source: *DTOe* xiv.1, 119.

89. JOSQUIN DES PRÈS: Agnus Dei. Josquin's historical and artistic position in the development of music may well be compared to that of his contemporary Raphael in the history of painting. Naturally, his artistic rank should not be judged from compositions like the present one, which is given here only in order to illustrate the use of canonic riddles in Flemish music, a trait which, although not without interest, has been overemphasized in modern writings. As indicated by the words "Ex una voce tres" (three voice parts out of one), this composition has only one notated part, which, however, leads to three rhythmically different parts when it is read in the three different mensurations given at the beginning. Compositions of this type are known as mensuration canons (see No. 92). Our example shows this interesting specimen in its original notation and in modern transcription. ¶ Source: *ApNPM*, p. 181.

90. JOSQUIN DES PRÈS: "Tu pauperum refugium." Josquin's "Tu pauperum refugium" (the second part of his motet "Magnus es tu, Domine") is one of numerous compositions from his pen which elevate him, more than anyone else, to the rank of the classical master of Renaissance music. It shows an admirable combination of spirituality and expressiveness, of variety and clarity, of technical mastery and simplicity of means as well as close reciprocity between text and music—in short, all those traits which make him the outstanding master of musical humanism or, in sixteenth-century terminology, of *musica reservata*. Incidentally, this composition contains many subtle examples of word paintings. ¶ Source: Complete edition (by Smijers), Bundel III, p. 93. ¶ Record: *GSE*, p. 242.

91. JOSQUIN DES PRÈS: "Faulte d'argent." The present example illustrates the French chanson of the early sixteenth century, a type which was destined to have a far-reaching influence upon the further course of music, leading later to the instrumental canzona (see Nos. 118, 136, 175) and ultimately to the sonata. Particularly noteworthy in this respect is the ternary form of the present composition, A B A (cf. the sections "Faulte," "Se ie le dis," and "Femme"). Another interesting feature is the canonic treatment of the contra-tenor and the quinta pars, the latter imitating the former in the lower fifth at a distance of three measures. For an organ adaptation of this chanson see No. 118. ¶ Source: Complete edition (by A. Smijers), "Wereldlijke Werken," Nr. 15.

92. PIERRE DE LA RUE. As yet little is known of the work of this composer, whose importance may well be con-siderably greater than is generally assumed today when his fame rests mainly on his mastery of the "intricacies of mensural notation." For this mastery the present example serves as an illustration. It is a mensuration canon (see No. 89), that is, a composition in which a single written line serves for two (or more) voice-parts, when the line is read in different mensurations. In the present case the melody of "L'Homme armé" is sung simultaneously in triple time (*tempus perfectum*) by the tenor and in duple time (*tempus imperfectum*) by the bass. ¶ Source: *Misse Petri de la Rue* (Petrucci, 1503).

93. PAULUS HOFHAIMER. Hofhaimer is the outstand-ing representative of the early Renaissance in Germany, as is Josquin in France. His compositions, mostly German part songs, show a typically German seriousness and depth of feeling. His "Mein's traurens ist" has the structure of the *Bar* (see Nos. 20 and 24), and is written in the Phrygian mode, which was frequently used in the period of Josquin (cf. Nos. 90 and 111). In the original edition (Georg Forster, *Ein Ausszug guter alter und neuer teutscher Liedlein . . .*, 1539) only the tenor has a text. ¶ Source: H. J. Moser, *Gesammelte Tonsätze Paul Hofhaimer's* (1929), p. 72.

94. GIACOMO FOGLIANO. After an interruption of two hundred years, caused, no doubt, by the loss of sources, the Italian laude (cf. No. 21) reappeared in the form of polyphonic compositions. The sixteenth-century laude are written in a simple chordal style, similar to that of the con-temporary frottole (cf. No. 95). A comparison of Fogliano's composition with the plainsong melody (*LU*, p. 1861) is recommended. ¶ Source: K. Jeppesen, *Die mehrstimmige italienische Laude um 1500* (1935), p. 163.

95. TWO FROTTOLE. The splendid vitality of the Italian Renaissance brought with it an extensive cultivation of secu-lar music. In the years from 1504 to 1514 the Venetian pub-lisher Petrucci issued eleven books of *Frottole*, that is, love songs composed in three or four parts which were greatly in vogue among the members of the North Italian courts, particularly at Mantua where Tromboncino lived. Most of the frottole are written in a form similar to that of the thirteenth-century ballata (or virelai; cf. Nos. 19 and 21). They consist of an initial refrain (*ripresa*, r), a number of stanzas (*piedi*, p), and a concluding refrain (*volta*, v) which has the same text and, except for a cadential extension, the same music as the ripresa. The arrangement of these sections

is: r p$_1$ v r p$_2$ v . . . or, perhaps, r p$_1$ v p$_2$ v . . . The musical scheme usually is

$$\overbrace{}^{r}\;\;\overbrace{}^{p}\;\;\overbrace{}^{v}$$
$$\text{A B} \quad \text{a a b} \quad \text{A}^{-}$$

(A^{-} is the same as A, except for a cadential extension.) ¶ Source: R. Schwartz, *Ottaviano Petrucci, Frottole* (1935), pp. 14, 37.

96. CANTO CARNASCIALESCO. The carnival songs of the early sixteenth century reflect the exuberant liveliness of the Italian Renaissance. They were sung by masked people standing in open carriages in a street procession, as is the custom to the present day in various Latin countries. The singers of the "Per scriptores" were disguised as scribes offer-ing their efficient services for the writing of bulls, a pun which was not lost on the audience at a time when the despatch of papal bulls was a notoriously slow procedure. ¶ Source: Joh. Wolf, *Sing- und Spielmusik aus älterer Zeit* (1931), p. 49.

97, 98. MILLAN, ENCINA. The rise of the Italian frottola is paralleled by that of the Spanish villancico of the period around 1500. About 450 such compositions, lyrical songs with instrumental accompaniment, are preserved in the so-called *Cancionero del palacio* of Madrid. Stylistic evidence seems to indicate a slightly earlier date for Millan (not to be con-fused with Luis de Milan, cf. No. 121) than for Juan Encina, also famous as a poet, whose songs figure largely among those of the Cancionero. Encina's songs, though generally of slighter value than the earlier ones, nevertheless are attractive examples of a popular style. They are mostly written in the form a b b a, derived from the French virelai (cf. No. 19), which was used as early as 1300 in the Spanish cantigas (cf. No. 22). In the "Durandarte" the two sections of music are repeated five times with new text, closing with the first sec-tion, on *Fine* (a b a b . . . a). ¶ Source: F. A. Barbieri, *Cancionero musical de los siglos XV y XVI* (1890), nos. 270, 343, 152, 22, 190.

99. TWO LUTE RICERCARS. The term ricercar, though usually understood to indicate an early type of fugue, actu-ally has a wider significance. It is the equivalent of our expression "study"—or some other term loose enough to embrace a considerable variety of instrumental styles and types (cf. Nos. 114, 116, 119, 136). The lute ricercars con-tained in Petrucci's lute books of 1507-08 are the earliest known pieces thus named. They are free studies in lute style designed to exploit the idiomatic resources of this instrument. No. 99a consists of two short sections, a sort of prelude (*tastar de corde*, touching of the strings) and the *ricercar dietro* (ricercar thereafter). A few notes obviously wrong in the original edition have been corrected. ¶ Sources: (a) Pe-trucci, *Intabulatura de lauto*, vol. IV (1508); (b) *Intabulatura* II (1507), fol. 46v.

100. ARNOLT SCHLICK: "Salve Regina." With Arnolt Schlick, the development of German organ music (cf. Nos.

81 and 84) came to an early culmination of great artistic significance. Spiritually and stylistically his compositions belong to a somewhat earlier period than that in which they were written, namely, to that of the late Gothic as represented by Ockeghem. Evidence of this connection is found in the strictly horizontal structure of the "Salve Regina," in the sustained notes of the cantus firmus, in the florid design of the contrapuntal parts which is largely free from the rational methods of the Renaissance. A noteworthy exception to the last statement is the imitative entrance of the three contrapuntal parts, each of which begins with the same "subject," if this term may be permitted for a musical idea which has little in common with a subject in the usual sense of the word. See also No. 139. ¶ Source: Arnolt Schlick, *Tabulaturen etlicher Lobgesang . . .* (1512), new edition by G. Harms (1924).

101. ARNOLT SCHLICK: "Maria zart." Among Schlick's organ pieces the "Maria zart" is the only one based on a German devotional hymn, all the others being adapted from the Latin liturgy of the Roman Church. This exceptional derivation is reflected in various features of the musical style. The melody is more tuneful and folk-like than the chants of plainsong. It differs from plainsong also in its clearly marked phrases, thus foreshadowing the Lutheran chorale which came to the fore some twenty years after Schlick. Of particular importance is the fact that in Schlick's organ composition this melody is used, not as a structural cantus firmus in evenly sustained notes, but as a freely exhibited soprano part, embellished by subtle ornamentations and supported by two contrapuntal parts which are remarkable for the exquisite clarity of their lines as well as for their most skillful incorporation of thematic material, either in the manner of canonic imitation or of *Vorimitation*. Literally, anticipating imitation, *Vorimitation* is the technical term for the imitative treatment of a chorale line (or of its initial motive), as a preparation to the full statement of the melody. ¶ Source: Same as No. 100.

102. TWO DANCES. The sixteenth century may fittingly be characterized as "the century of the dance." Encouraged by a freer attitude towards the authority of the Church, people of all classes—nobility, burghers, and peasants—took to dancing with an abandon for which there is hardly a parallel in the history of mankind. The two dances given here represent an early type which occurs in Spanish, German, Italian, and French sources around and after 1500, in the Italian known as *bassa danza* and in the French as *basse danse*. These dances are in slow triple meter, with longer note values in the lower parts, and lively passages and figurations in the upper part. Most of them clearly belong to the category of tenor dances, that is, dances in which the tenor forms the basic part. Such a tenor is easily discernible in the "Alta" of the Spanish composer F. de la Torre, while in Weck's "Spanyöler Tancz" the same melody ("Spagna") occurs in the soprano. Weck's composition consists of two dances (*Hopper dancz* means jumping dance), as is fre-

quently the case in the dance literature of the sixteenth century. ¶ Sources: (a) F. A. Barbieri, *Cancionero musical del los siglos XV y XVI* (1890), no. 439; (b) W. Merian, *Der Tanz in den deutschen Tabulaturbüchern . . . des 16. Jahrhunderts* (1927), p. 48.

103. ENGLISH DOMPE. This interesting composition is contained in a manuscript in the British Museum which was written about 1525, the earliest preserved source of English keyboard music aside from the Robertsbridge Codex (see No. 58). "Dump" is believed to be a lamenting and sorrowful type of English or Irish song. Shakespeare, however, mentions "doleful dumps" and "merry dumps" (*Romeo and Juliet*, IV, 4). The present dance is particularly interesting because of the ostinato character of the accompaniment. In a way, it can be considered as a series of continuous variations on a tonic-dominant harmony as a "theme." Thus it belongs in the same category with the passacaglia or chaconne of the seventeenth century. ¶ Source: Brit. Mus. *Roy. App. 58*.

104. FRENCH PAVANE. The pavane is a courtly dance, probably of Spanish origin, which around 1500 superseded the basse danse (see No. 102). Aside from a few early examples in triple meter, the pavane is always in slow duple meter. It is frequently followed by a *Nachtanz*, the galliard, in quicker triple meter. A special trait of the pavane is the structure in three clearly marked sections, A B C, each of which is repeated. This form is shown by the present example as well as by most of the English pavanes dating from the end of the century (see Nos. 137, 179). ¶ Source: Pierre Attaingnant, *Quatorze gaillardes, neuf pavanes . . .* (1529), facsimile edition by E. Bernoulli (1914), p. 73.

105. HANS NEUSIEDLER. Among the numerous German lute composers of the sixteenth century, Hans Neusiedler is, perhaps, the most important. His "Hoftanz" (court dance) is similar in rhythm and style to the "Spanyöler Tancz" by Hans Weck (No. 102b). His "Der Juden Tanz" (The Jew's Dance) is one of the most remarkable specimens of sixteenth-century music. Shrill dissonances, otherwise unheard of before the adventurous experiments of twentieth-century music, result from the daring use of two conflicting tonal realms (bitonality), D-sharp in the melody against E-natural in the harmony. They produce an extremely realistic picture, not lacking a touch of satire. Each dance is followed by a *Nachtanz* ("Hupf-auf," literally jump-up, i.e., jumping dance) which is a rhythmic variant of the main dance. Such dances were called *Proportz*, a name which is derived from the proportions of mensural notation (*proportio tripla*). ¶ Sources: *DTOe* XVIII.2, 34 and 58 (cf. also the remark in *ApNPM*, p. 78).

106. ANTOINE DE FEVIN. Fevin, if not a pupil of Josquin, certainly was a "felix Jodoci aemulator" (a successful follower of Josquin), to use Glarean's words. His style is admirable for its clarity, simplicity, and expressiveness. The present example illustrates, among other things, the

practice of temporarily reducing the number of voices from the customary four to two (or three), in the present case for the second Agnus Dei. This method, obviously an effort to wrest some contrast from the uniform medium of a choral group, is frequently found in the fifteenth century (see, for example, Nos. 56, 64), but was seldom used after Josquin. The Agnus III illustrates another characteristic trait of the Josquin period, namely, the imitation in paired voice parts (cf. the passages "Agnus Dei" and "dona nobis pacem"). ¶ Source: *Liber quindecim missarum* (new edition in ExMM, p. 116).

107. CLÉMENT JANEQUIN. The present example is one of the several program chansons which made Janequin one of the most popular composers of the sixteenth century, and which constitute an early example of true secular style. Although of a somewhat limited artistic significance, these compositions are remarkable for their technical cleverness and stylistic elegance, qualities which, in combination with their witty and somewhat frivolous texts, easily account for their success. ¶ Source: Cl. Janequin, *Chansons* (new edition in ExMM, p. 105).

108. THOMAS STOLTZER. Stoltzer is a member of that group of early sixteenth-century composers who came under the influence of the Lutheran Reformation (1519) and contributed towards the musical repertory of the newly founded Protestant Church in Germany, thus laying the foundation for the splendid development of the Protestant chorale which was to become a cornerstone of German music through the time of J. S. Bach. In the present example, which has the chorale melody (cantus firmus) in the tenor, the *Vorimitation* of the initial phrase and the chordal style of the passage "Christ will unser Trost sein" may be noticed. ¶ Source: *DdT* xxxiv, 26.

109. LUDWIG SENFL: "Salutatio prima." Senfl was a pupil of Isaac, whom he succeeded as director of the court chapel of the Emperor Maximilian I. His "Salutatio prima" offers a good illustration of the imitative motet style of the sixteenth century, with its quickly changing points of imitation. It also illustrates the considerable degree of freedom with which this principle was applied. ¶ Source: *DTB* iii.2, p. 103.

110. LUDWIG SENFL: "Da Jakob nu das Kleid ansah." Senfl's German songs run the whole gamut of musical expression, from rugged humor to profound seriousness. In the present example the story of Jacob's despair at seeing the bloodstained coat of his son Joseph finds a musical expression fully as moving as the words of Scripture. ¶ Source: *DdT* xxxiv, 180.

111. TWO SETTINGS OF A GERMAN CHORALE. Johann Walter's setting of the German chorale "Aus tiefer Not," if compared with Stoltzer's "Christ ist erstanden" (No. 108), illustrates the tendency toward less elaborate methods of musical composition in this genre. The chorale is still in the tenor, but the other voices move along in a fairly simple chordal style, such as became universally adopted for the chorale in the seventeenth century. Bruck treats the chorale melody as a free canon between the tenor and the soprano, a method which is found in a number of Bach's organ chorales. ¶ Sources: (a) Joh. Walter, *Wittembergisch geistlich Gesangbuch* (1524), new edition by Eitner, p. 10; (b) *DTOe* xxxiv, 104. ¶ Record: (b) *Decca-20160*.

112. JOHN TAVERNER. The development of English music, which suffered a considerable lapse after Dunstable (cf. No. 61), again rose to new heights during the sixteenth century. Taverner is the oldest in the T-triad of early Tudor composers who brought about this development, the others being Christopher Tye and Thomas Tallis (see No. 127) The composition of masses based on an English folk tune, "The Western Wynde," was almost as popular among English musicians as was the similar use of "L'Homme armé" in France. In the "Benedictus" from Taverner's *Mass the Western Wynde* the tune is stated three times in full: first in the soprano, then twice in the tenor. Of special interest is the frequent use of a small motive, f e d c . . . (see measure 5 of the tune), as an integral part of the contrapuntal web, particularly in the soprano. The use of such "ostinato" motives seems to have been a peculiar trait of English music during the earlier part of the sixteenth century (see No. 120b). ¶ Source: *Tudor Church Music*, i, 20.

113. ADRIAN WILLAERT: "Victimae paschali laudes." Willaert was a Flemish musician who settled in Venice, where he founded a school of composition including among others Andrea Gabrieli, Claudio Merulo, and Giovanni Gabrieli and known as the Venetian School. Very few of his compositions have been made accessible in modern editions. No doubt, further studies will prove him to be an even greater master than is generally assumed today. In his "Victimae paschali laudes" the plainsong melody of this celebrated sequence (cf. No. 16b) is used as a cantus firmus, first in the Sextus which sings the initial phrase only, then in the Quintus which has it entire. Our example shows only the Prima pars of the motet. ¶ Source: A. Willaert, *Musica nova* (1559).

114. NIKOLAUS GOMBERT. Gombert was a Flemish master who was a pupil of Josquin. His "Super flumina" offers a good example for the study of the classical motet style of the sixteenth century. The basic principle of this style is the use of short "points of imitation" for small divisions of the text, each of these "points" being based on a different subject. Usually the conclusion of one point (e.g., "Super flumina") overlaps with the beginning of the next ("illic sedimus"). While most of the divisions of the text are treated in this fashion, there are some in which the method is modified as, for example, in "illic sedimus," which has one subject for the soprano and alto, another for the tenor and bass, or in "Quomodo cantabimus," in which a more har-

monic style is used. The influence of Josquin may be seen in the degree of poignancy which exists between the text and the music. ¶ Source: N. Gombert, *Musica quatuor vocum* (1541).

115. ADRIAN WILLAERT: Ricercar. Willaert's importance in the field of instrumental music has long been recognized. His ricercars conform to the current interpretation of this term as a designation for instrumental pieces in the imitative style of the sixteenth-century motet; in fact, they come much closer to the true motet style than, for example, the ricercars by Cavazzoni (cf. No. 116). One reason for this is that they are not written for the organ, as is frequently assumed, but for three melody instruments, such as viols or recorders. A vocalizing (i.e., textless) execution by three solo singers is also a distinct possibility as is indicated in the title inscription of the original edition: "appropriati per cantare e sonare d'ogni sorte di stromenti." (*Stromenti* means here ensemble instruments such as viols or recorders, not organ or harpsichord.) ¶ Source: A. Willaert, *Fantasie, Ricercari, Contrapunti . . .* (1559), Ricercar decimo.

116. GIROLAMO CAVAZZONI: Ricercar. Cavazzoni holds a central position in the early development of organ music. Judging from a remark in the preface to his organ books of 1542/43, he was a young man when he published them. Nevertheless the compositions contained therein are landmarks in the history of organ music, being equally remarkable for their novelty and for their artistic perfection. Cavazzoni's ricercars are the first organ ricercars proper, that is, organ compositions written in the imitative style of the sixteenth-century motet. It should be noticed, however, that these organ ricercars are considerably more independent of their model than the ensemble ricercars by Willaert (cf. No. 115). The most important difference is that the short points of imitation, which form the basis of motet style (cf. No. 114), are frequently extended into lengthy sections, each of which presents its subject in numerous statements. Consequently, the number of these sections is considerably less than that of the points in a motet of comparable length. Thus, Cavazzoni's ricercars may well be said to consist of four or five "fugues," a statement which would rarely, if ever, apply to a sixteenth-century motet. Another stylistic peculiarity worthy of note is the free-voice writing (German, *Freistimmigkeit*), entailing free change in the number of voice-parts, omission of rests in places where they would be required from the point of view of strict counterpoint, use of five-voice chords within a four-voice texture, etc. This free treatment is a characteristic by-product of the emergence of solo instrumental music, for keyboard instruments as well as for lute or viola da gamba (see No. 119). ¶ Source: G. Cavazzoni, *Intavolatura cioè recercari canzoni himni magnificati* (1542/43), new edition by G. Benvenuti.

117. GIROLAMO CAVAZZONI: *Missa Apostolorum.* The organ music of the sixteenth century includes an ex-traordinarily large repertory of liturgical organ compositions designed to take the traditional place of plainsong. Our example shows that even in the celebration of the Mass the organ took a prominent part. It is based on the *Missa Apostolorum* (Mass No. IV, also known as *Missa Cunctipotens;* see No. 15), and consists of a number of short organ pieces for the Kyrie and the Gloria of this Mass. A comparison with the plainsong Mass (*LU,* p. 25) will show that the musical performance of the Mass was not purely instrumental, but consisted of an alternation of organ music and plainsong, the latter being used for all the sections ("Gloria in excelsis," "Laudamus te," "Adoramus te," etc.) which are not included in the organ composition. Another evidence of this alternating performance is the fact that the "second Kyrie" (after the Christe) is designated in the original source as "Chyrie quartus." Evidently, the first Kyrie, after being played on the organ, was sung twice in plainsong, so that the so-called "second Kyrie" actually becomes the fourth. Naturally, the same method applies to the Christe and the last Kyrie, in accordance with the traditional structure of this chant. ¶ Source: Same as No. 116.

118. GIROLAMO CAVAZZONI: "Falte d'argens." This composition is another example of the early instrumental canzona, the origin of which can be traced back as far as Obrecht (see No. 78). As a comparison with No. 91 readily shows, this is an organ composition based on the themes of Josquin's "Faulte d'argent," a French chanson (hence the name "canzona francese" or, simply, "canzona"). Later composers wrote original compositions of the same type, transferring the lively character, the tone-repeating motifs, and the sectional structure of the French chanson to the organ as well as to instrumental ensembles (see Nos. 136, 175). The organ canzona (*canzona d'organo*) is the most important forerunner of the seventeenth-century fugue, while the ensemble canzona (*canzona da sonare*) developed into the Baroque chamber sonata (see No. 136). ¶ Source: Same as No. 116.

119. SILVESTRO GANASSI. Ganassi is the author of the *Regola Rubertina* (1542/43), the earliest treatise dealing with the playing of the viol and the bass viol (viola da gamba). This book is particularly interesting for its numerous musical examples, the earliest extant compositions for these instruments. Ganassi's ricercars for the viola da gamba are not, of course, modeled after the imitative style of the motet, but are "studies" similar in character and purpose to the early lute ricercars (see No. 99). The second of the two examples given here is remarkable for its extended use of double-stops. ¶ Source: Ganassi, *Regola Rubertina* (facsimile edition by M. Schneider, 1924), Libro I, no. 1, and Libro II, no. 2.

120. JOHN REDFORD. Redford is the most outstanding among the numerous English organ composers before the "virginalists" Byrd, Bull, Gibbons, and their colleagues. Apparently, from what is known to us, he devoted himself exclusively to the cultivation of liturgical organ music. Our

first example (a) is based on the melody of the Ambrosian hymn "Veni redemptor gentium." This melody is not used in its original form, but is freely amplified by inserted notes, a procedure reminiscent of the discant cantus firmi of the Dufay period (see No. 65). The "Lucem tuam" (b) is interesting as another example of the ostinato technique which has been encountered in Taverner's Mass (see No. 112). In the present case, the ostinato motif occurs in both contrapuntal parts, soprano as well as bass. ¶ Source: C. Pfatteicher, *John Redford* (1934), pp. 61 and 18.

121. LUIS DE MILAN. Examples 121 to 124 illustrate the Spanish lute music of the sixteenth century. It is interesting to notice that the flowering period of Spanish music preceded that of Spanish literature by fifty years (Cervantes, 1547–1633; Lope de Vega, 1567–1635), and that of Spanish painting by one hundred years (Velasquez, 1599–1660; Murillo, 1617–1682). Milan's *Libro de musica de vihuela de mano* (Music Book for the Lute) of 1535 contains forty fantasias, or compositions in a free idiomatic lute style consisting of chords, running passages, and pseudo-polyphonic elements. The present fantasia (his No. 17) belongs to a group (Nos. 10 to 18) in which the polyphonic or imitative element is reduced to a minimum, while the other two traits are predominant. The special nature of these fantasias is clearly pointed out by Milan, and it is particularly interesting to notice that he repeatedly admonishes the reader to play these fantasias in a free tempo, "es redobles apriesa y la consonancia a espacio" (the ornamented passages fast, and the harmonies slowly) adding that "este musica no tiene mucho respecto al compas" (cf. pp. 24, 36, and 48 of the modern edition). This is the first instance in music history of a deliberately free tempo, and Milan's insistence on this point is easily explained by the novelty of the procedure. ¶ Source: Milan, *Libro de musica* (new edition by L. Schrade, 1927), p. 42.

122. LUIS DE NARVAEZ. The variations contained in Narvaez's lute book of 1538 are the earliest extant examples of the variation form. They clearly demonstrate the high standard to which this form had developed in Spain at a time when it was as yet unknown in other countries. Here follow translations of the various original inscriptions: First variation. Here begins the final [cadenza].—Second variation with two upper parts above the tenor.—Third variation in two parts; it should be played in a fast meter in order to make it sound well.—Fourth variation in proportion [i.e., *proportio tripla,* triple time].—Fifth variation; the plainsong in the soprano.—Here begins the final [cadenza].—Sixth variation; the plainsong in the tenor. ¶ Source: Narvaez, *Los seys libros del Delphin de musica* (1538).

123. MIGUEL DE FUENLLANA. The lute books of Fuenllana and of Valderravano (see No. 124) contain a great number of solo songs with lute accompaniment. These are the earliest examples of accompanied song in the modern sense of the word, in contrast to the fifteenth-century type of polyphonic chamber music written for one singer and two melody instruments (see Nos. 67, 69, 71, etc.). In these Spanish sixteenth-century songs the emphasis is clearly on the vocal part, and the lute provides a subsidiary accompaniment consisting of chords and modest figurations, while in the fifteenth-century songs the solo singer is coupled with instrumental participants of equal importance. The "Paseá-base el rey" was a Spanish folksong, as appears from the fact that various lute composers have used the same melody, providing different accompaniments (e.g., Fuenllana, Pisador, and Narvaez). ¶ Source: G. Morphy, *Les Luthistes espagnoles du xvie siècle* (1902), II, 198. ¶ Record: *AS-17* (*GSE,* p. 555.)

124. ANRIQUEZ DE VALDERRAVANO. The present example of Spanish lute variations is based on a theme which has been used by practically all the Spanish lutenists, as well as by the organ master Cabezon. The title "Guardame las vacas" suggests that the theme is a Spanish folksong which was very popular at that time. Its melody is essentially a descending group of four notes. Of particular interest is the fact that the "Guardame" melody is identical with the so-called "Romanesca" which was used by numerous Italian Baroque composers (Trabaci, Frescobaldi) as a theme for variations. Moreover, it forms the melodic basis for the passamezzo antico (see No. 154). ¶ Source: Valderravano, *Libro llamado Silva de Sirenas* (1547).

125. CLEMENS NON PAPA. This Flemish composer is justly famous for the expressiveness of his melodies, the clarity of his style, and his advanced treatment of the harmonic idiom. It will be noticed that the basic method of motet technique, the principle of points of imitation, is used in this composition with considerably greater freedom than by Gombert, for instance (see No. 114). For example, the phrases "audita est" and "et ululatus" show little, if any, trace of this method. As regards the harmonic point of view, the Neapolitan sixth in measure 5 of system 4 may be noticed. The composition is not based on the plainsong melody of the text (cf. *LU,* p. 430). ¶ Source: C. Proske, *Musica divina,* tomus II.

126. TWO SETTINGS OF PSALM 35. While the German Reformation under Luther led to the establishment of the German chorale (see Nos. 108, 111), the Genevan Reformation under Calvin (1541) rejected such texts on the ground that they were man-made and not "inspired." Instead, the psalms were chosen as the only source of texts for congregational singing, and the Genevan Psalter of 1562, containing metrical paraphrases of the psalms in the French language, was officially adopted by the Protestant churches in Switzerland, France, and the Netherlands. The simpler style for Psalter texts is illustrated by that shown in No. 132; the Goudimel and Claude le Jeune examples given here represent a more elaborate treatment. ¶ Sources: (a) Claude Goudimel, *1er. Fasc. des 150 Psaumes* (ExMM, I, 51); (b) Claude le Jeune, *Dodecacorde* (ExMM, II, 26).

127. THOMAS TALLIS. The "Audivi vocem" is a responsorium ("pro pluribus virginibus"; cf. the *Processionale monasticum*, 1893, p. 236). As explained under Nos. 12–14, the responsoria, as well as the graduals and alleluias, are chants in which sections for soloists alternate with others for the full choir. As early as the thirteenth century the practice became established of replacing the solo sections by polyphonic compositions, while the choir sections continued to be sung in plainsong (see Nos. 26ff). It is interesting to observe that this practice survived as late as the sixteenth century, the present composition being an example in point. There are three solo sections in this chant, namely, "Audivi vocem," "Media nocte . . . venit," and "Gloria patri." Tallis, however, composed only the first two of these, probably because the Church did not permit the Gloria patri to be replaced by a polyphonic setting. Very likely the polyphonic sections were sung, not by the whole choir, but by a few picked soloists. ¶ Source: *Tudor Church Music*, VI, 90.

128. CRISTOBAL MORALES. Although the Flemish style became the international musical language of the sixteenth century, this language naturally was colored to a certain extent by the national characteristics of the different countries. In Spain it frequently adopted a subjective, occasionally even dramatic, expression. Morales' motet "Emendemus in melius" is an impressive example of this spirit. The dramatic element may be observed here in the grim reiteration "Memento homo" which interrupts at intervals the petition "Emendemus in melius." ¶ Source: D. H. Eslava, *Lira sacro-Hispana* (1869).

129–131. COSTANZO FESTA, IACOB ARCADELT, CIPRIANO DE RORE. The three compositions given here illustrate the early history of the madrigal, the most important type of sixteenth-century secular music. The madrigal developed from earlier types of Italian secular music, such as the frottola (see No. 95), under the refining influence of literary men like Cardinal Bembo, and of Flemish composers living in Italy, mainly Verdelot, Willaert, and Arcadelt. The earliest madrigals are written in a very simple homophonic style, as illustrated by the "Quando ritrova," by Festa, the first native composer of madrigals. Arcadelt's "Voi ve n'andate," published in 1539, represents a considerably more advanced type which clearly shows the influence of the contemporary motet but also includes expressive elements proper to the madrigal, as for instance, the impatient urge of the passage "Ma struggendo." This tendency is carried considerably farther in Cipriano de Rore's "Da le belle contrade" with its exciting exclamations "T'en vai," its daring change of harmony at "Ahi crud' amor," its word-painting of the "Iterando amplessi," and its prophetic use of chromaticism. The parallel unisons in score 4, measure 6, of page 143 will doubtless be noted. They occur in the edition from which the editors drew this piece, and they are certainly questionable. ¶ Sources: (129) Brit. Mus. *Add.* 34071, ff. 28a and b; (130) and (131) F. Blume, *Das Chorwerk*, Heft V, nos. 4 and 7. ¶ Record (129) *GSE*, p. 167.

132. LOUIS BOURGEOIS. Bourgeois played a leading role in the development of Reformed Church music. From about 1541 to 1557 he was the musical editor of the Genevan Psalter. His polyphonic settings of the Psalter texts are the earliest. They are almost uniformly in a single chordal style, one note to a syllable. Most of them employ the Psalter tune in the tenor, and the present example is one of these. (See also the commentary on No. 126.) ¶ Source: Douen, *C. Marot et le Psautier Huguenot*, II, 83.

133. ANTONIO DE CABEZON: "Versos del sexto tono." Cabezon, the Spanish organ master of the sixteenth century, has repeatedly been associated with Bach, and in this case the association has considerable significance. It points to an inner relationship between these two masters, who, much as they differ in their forms and styles, are close to each other in their musical spirituality, in their profundity and austerity of thought, in their seriousness of purpose, and—last but not least—in their mastery of technical means. The "Versos" are organ versets, that is, short organ pieces designed to be used in connection with the singing of the psalms. The monotony inherent in the traditional psalm-singing of plainsong (cf. No. 11), with its frequent repetition of the same short recitation formula, led in the sixteenth century to the practice of replacing the even-numbered verses by polyphonic settings, either for chorus or for the organ. Cabezon wrote for each psalm tone four versets which have the cantus firmus (*canto llano*) successively in the soprano (*tiple*), alto, tenor, and bass (*contrabaxo*). ¶ Source: F. Pedrell, *Hispaniae schola musica sacra* (1895–98), III, 27.

134. ANTONIO DE CABEZON: "Diferencias Cavallero." It has been pointed out previously (see No. 122) that Spain played a leading role in the development of the variation form. Cabezon's variations for keyboard instrument offer an even more convincing evidence of this fact than the Spanish lute variations which stand at the beginning of the development of this form. The theme of Cabezon's "Diferencias Cavallero," evidently an ancient Spanish folksong, is interesting because of its rhythmic structure. Although it is notated in 2/2 throughout, its musical rhythm projects itself more clearly if the two opening quarter-notes are regarded as an up beat, and if the subsequent first half of the theme is read according to the following metrical scheme: 2/2, 2/2, 3/2, 3/2, 3/1, a scheme which is repeated identically for the concluding half of the tune. Cabezon's variations are all contrapuntal paraphrases of a cantus firmus, but within the limits of this style they offer an admirable variety of musical ideas. It is interesting to notice that in all his variation works Cabezon connects the variations by transitional passages, a happy device which is rarely encountered elsewhere. ¶ Source: Same as for No. 133, vol. VIII, p. 3. ¶ Record: *AS-69* (*GSE*, p. 92).

135. ANDREA GABRIELI: "Intonazione settimo tono." The "Intonazioni" of Andrea Gabrieli are festive organ preludes written in the style of his toccatas. While the toccatas

are not free from monotony, this flaw is avoided in the considerably shorter intonations. ¶ Source: *Intonationi d'organo di Andrea Gabrieli et di Giov. suo nipote . . .* (1593).

136. ANDREA GABRIELI: "Ricercare del 12° tono." This composition, although originally entitled "ricercar," actually is a canzona, as appears from the lively character of its themes as well as from the fact that entire sections are repeated, a procedure which is frequent in canzonas but foreign to the ricercar style. It is written, not for organ, but for a quartet of instruments such as viols, and therefore represents one of the earliest examples of the *canzona da sonare,* a type which, during the seventeenth century, gradually led to the sonata. Our example clearly shows the sections in contrasting rhythms and styles which eventually became the separate movements of the sonata. ¶ Source: *Madrigali et ricercari di Andrea Gabrieli . . .* (1589), new edition in *Istituzioni e monumenti dell' arte musicale italiana* (1931ff), I, 86. ¶ Record: *Columbia-70366D.*

137. CLAUDE GERVAISE. Gervaise's "Danseries" of 1550–1555 are a large collection of dances for chamber ensembles of four or five instruments. This example illustrates three important types of sixteenth-century dance music, the basse danse (c. 1475-1525), the pavane (c. 1525-1600), and the allemande, which appeared around 1550 and was adopted into the suite of the Baroque period. The pavane of the present example shows the typical structure of this dance, in three sections (cf. Nos. 104, 179). The galliard, as was often the case in the sixteenth century, uses the same melody and approximately the same harmonies as the pavane, the chief difference being a change from duple to triple meter (*proportz;* cf. No. 105). ¶ Source: H. Expert, *Maîtres musiciens de la renaissance française,* XXIII, 4, 18, 48. ¶ Record: *AS-5 (GSE,* p. 180).

138. CLAUDE LE JEUNE. The present composition is an example of *vers mesuré.* The vers mesuré (ascribed to Antoine de Baïf) originated in French literary humanism as a reaction against what is called *vers rimé* with its regularly recurring accents. It is based not on the regular meters imposed by rhymed poetry but on the classical system of long and short feet. Musicians like Claude le Jeune were strongly influenced by these literary tendencies. They composed music to the poetic texts in a rather plain chordal style (familiar style) and in a rhythm which exactly reproduces the declamation of the text, by giving the strong syllables twice the duration of the weak syllables. ¶ Source: Claude le Jeune, *Le Printemps* (1603), new edition in H. Expert, *Les Maîtres musiciens de la renaissance française,* XXXV, 91.

139. FRANCISCO GUERRERO. The "Salve Regina" is the most celebrated of the four antiphons of the Blessed Virgin Mary (antiphons B. M. V.). Its text and plainsong melody are ascribed to Hermannus Contractus (1013-1054). This antiphon is traditionally sung by alternating choruses, and the ancient practice was retained in the polyphonic compositions of the "Salve" which usually include only the even-numbered (or, in other cases, the odd-numbered) verses, the others being sung *alternatim* in plainsong. A comparison with the plainsong melody (*LU,* p. 276) shows that the polyphonic sections of Guerrero's "Salve" are not freely composed, but are polyphonic paraphrases of the chant. ¶ Source: F. Pedrell, *Hispaniae schola musica sacra* (1894), II, 48.

140. GIOVANNI PALESTRINA: Agnus Dei I. Palestrina represents the culmination of the Flemish style of church composition as expressed in modal counterpoint and in vocality suggestive of the melodic flow and rhythmic flexibility of plainsong. The quality which makes Palestrina's music preëminent in its period is its abstraction, its avoidance of those technical resources which in the sixteenth century were beginning to be applied to secular style in particular— a marked pulse, extensive chromaticism, sharp dissonance, and expressive melody. After Palestrina, Roman Catholic composers began to cultivate a less pure style. The *Missa Papae Marcelli* (composed about 1560) is notable for its flawless counterpoint and for the beauty and dignity of its musical expression. ¶ Source: Complete edition (Haberl), XI, 149. ¶ Record: *Victor-35944.*

141. GIOVANNI PALESTRINA: "Sicut cervus." The initial theme, to the words "Sicut . . . aquarum," is remarkable for its individual design and expressive quality, as are other motives used in the continuation of the motet. The division of a motet into two sections (Prima pars, Secunda pars) is a very frequent procedure in sixteenth-century composition. It is used particularly in connection with texts of "antiphonal" structure, such as psalm verses, which usually fall into two halves expressing the same thought in different ways. ¶ Source: Complete edition, V, 148. ¶ Records: *GSE,* p. 340; *Victor-20898.*

142. GIOVANNI PALESTRINA: "Alla riva del Tebro." Palestrina devoted himself chiefly to the field of sacred music, and his madrigals are in one sense a witness to his preoccupation with church style, in that they employ only to a modest degree the technical resources which were becoming definitely associated with secular musical method. In fact they are hardly more "expressive" than some of the motets of his colleagues Nanini and Victoria, and they never approach either in technique or in spirit the more "modern" madrigals of Marenzio and Gesualdo. Yet they are not written in Palestrina's own church style. Theirs is a beauty which results from a combination of technical perfection, reserve, and a profound sensitiveness to certain aspects of secular expression to which by nature he seems to have been drawn. In the present example, the expressive descending melody for the closing words "Ahi . . . sorte" should be particularly noticed. ¶ Source: Complete edition, XXVIII, 105. ¶ Record: *AS-47 (GSE,* p. 338).

143, 144. ORLANDO DI LASSO: "Requiem aeternam" and Penitential Psalm. Lasso, sometimes called the last great Netherlander of the Golden Age of choral music, represents the consummation of one aspect of a technique (Netherlands) which dominated musical thought for at least a hundred years. The harmonies underlying his counterpoint often move more rapidly than Palestrina's; there is, too, more attention to color, so that all in all the effect of the music is likely to be more emotional than is the case with Palestrina. The *Missa pro defunctis* and the Penitential Psalms are generally accepted as belonging among Lasso's highest achievements, representing, as they do, complete mastery of contrapuntal and expressive resource. Certainly they long have been considered as models in the study of sixteenth-century choral counterpoint. ¶ Sources: (143) O. Lassus, *Patrocinium musices* (1589); (144) O. di Lasso, *Septem psalmi poenitentiales* III (ed. Breitkopf und Härtel). ¶ Record: (143) *Victor-13560*.

145. ORLANDO DI LASSO: "Bon jour, mon cœur." Lasso's genius was not limited to the sacred field, for his secular pieces enjoy great renown and are still frequently performed. The texts embody a wide variety of ideas, and each is accorded a most appropriate musical treatment, characteristic of Lasso's versatility as a composer. Following a custom of the period which permitted the choice of some choral piece, often a madrigal, for conversion to an instrumental medium, the English composer Peter Philips has transformed Lasso's "Bon jour, mon cœur" into a piece for harpsichord. In transcriptions of this type, the notes of the melody of the original choral composition were retained, and these were surrounded by passages appropriate to the technique of the instrument on which the selection was to be performed. This process was known as "coloration." Only the opening of Philips' version is here reproduced but it will suffice to make the method clear. ¶ Source: (a) O. di Lasso, *Complete Works*, XII, 100; (b) *Fitzwilliam Virginal Book* (new edition by Fuller Maitland and Barclay Squire), I, 317.

146. MADRIGAL WITH PARODY MASS. A very frequent procedure in the sixteenth-century composition of masses was the use of musical material borrowed from other pieces—chansons, motets, or madrigals. It is to this technique that the term "parody mass" refers. Philipp de Monte's *Missa super Cara la vita* is based on a madrigal by Jacob van Werth. A comparison of the Sanctus with the madrigal will show to what extent the musical substance of the latter is incorporated into the former. Aside from the initial motive, various others are used, "ch'altra fiamma" ("Dominus Deus") and "in tanto tempo" ("Pleni sunt caeli"), for instance. ¶ Source: Ch. van den Borren, *Opera Philippi de Monte*, vol. XXI.

147. GUILLAUME COSTELEY. This charming Christmas song, abounding in originality and vitality, shows the French school of the sixteenth century at its very best. It should be noticed that this chanson is an example (no doubt one of the earliest) of the modern rondo form, characterized by the alternation of a recurrent refrain (in the present case,

"Allon, gay, gay") with various couplets (episodes). No less remarkable and advanced is the change from the minor to the major mode for the last statement of the refrain. ¶ Source: H. Expert, *Les Maîtres musiciens de la renaissance française* (G. Costeley, *Musique*, I, 65). ¶ Record: *AS-45* (*GSE*, p. 120).

148. JACOBUS DE KERLE. This motet illustrates, among other things, the gradual increase of the purely chordal (homophonic) style in the technique of composition during the latter part of the sixteenth century. The truly polyphonic and imitative texture of the beginning is abandoned, at the words "adjuva nos" and "et libera," for one which, although still imitative, emphasizes the harmonic rather than the melodic element; and the final section, to the words "propter nomen," is plainly chordal. Not unworthy of notice, too, is the literal repetition in this final section of an entire passage. Regarding chordal style in general, it may be said that where the words are particularly poignant or of special liturgical import, the use of chordal writing clearly emphasizes their significance. ¶ Source: C. Proske, *Musica divina*, II, 91.

149. TOMÁS LUIS DE VICTORIA. Victoria, a Spaniard, was a distinguished member of the Roman school of church composition, and numbered both Palestrina and Nanini among his colleagues. Reference has already been made to the extraordinary differences in technique and expressiveness that occur in the music of certain members of the Roman group (see No. 142). The melodic freedom, harmonic richness, and emotional power that are to be found in Nanini's work are also a feature of Victoria's writing. But the latter seems occasionally to embody a quality which transcends personal feeling and approaches the dramatic. The sixteenth-century ideal of vocality was best expressed in the constantly moving melodic line; and No. 149 will be found, in the main, to conform to that ideal. Where, however, there occurs a single word like "dolor," or even a whole passage such as "attendite universi populi," which is in a sense crucial and which claims the particular attention of the hearer, Victoria employs the dramatic device of the repeated note, used so effectively by Monteverdi and later opera composers. ¶ Source: Complete edition (by F. Pedrell), I, 27. ¶ Record: *GSE*, p. 498.

150. WILLIAM BYRD. An appreciation of William Byrd as one of the overtopping figures among sixteenth-century church composers has been delayed, owing partly to the inherited and now happily discredited tradition that no good musical thing could come out of England and partly to the long-standing conviction that Palestrina was so far superior to all others of his era—with the possible exception of Lasso—that all comparison was futile. Dependence on plainsong as a model for vocal procedure was never as great in England as on the Continent. In its place is to be found preoccupation with a type of lyricism that is wholly English and utterly in accord with the innermost nature of the human voice. This, together with a highly effective choral technique and a singularly subtle harmonic method reinforced by diversified

and telling rhythms, accords Byrd's music a unique position. The coda on the word "Alleluia" is characteristic. Byrd was fond, once the text had been fully set, of dispatching the singers on an excursion devoted to some word like "Amen" or "Alleluia" which, by its nature, invited vocal expansion. These codas, beautiful to the hearer and enthralling to the singer, are gems of choral art. ¶ Source: *Tudor Church Music*, VII, 318.

151. WILLIAM BYRD: "Christ rising again." This is an example of the so-called verse anthem, that is, one in which sections for full chorus alternate with others for accompanied solo voice or voices as well as with purely instrumental sections. This type, which became established in the late sixteenth century, is one of the various indications of the general trend towards introducing into music the element of contrast, a trend which became one of the basic characteristics of Baroque music (*stile concertato*). The beginning of the present composition affords one of the numerous examples of word painting, in the "rising" motives of the instruments as well as the voices. ¶ Source: W. Byrd, *Songs of Sundry Natures* . . . (1589), new ed. by E. H. Fellowes, *The English Madrigal School*, xv, 280.

152. GIOVANNI MARIA NANINI. Nanini is one of the first in the long line of musicians collectively referred to as the Roman School. Among the members of this group in Nanini's time was Palestrina, who, compared with Nanini, seems very much the conservative. Opulence of texture, chromaticism, expressive melody, all these and more are frequently to be found in the sacred music of Nanini. That his daring entitles him to rank among the musical prophets is borne out by a remark of the late Sir Donald Tovey that surprise is always imminent in Nanini's music. This, however, is but one facet of his work. He was also a finished technician according to the best Netherlands standards, yet his technical proficiency was invariably the servant of beauty. The example here presented, a strict canon between soprano and bass, is intended to illustrate this latter aspect of Nanini's genius. ¶ Source: A. Proske, *Musica divina*, II, 57.

153. CLAUDIO MERULO. The toccata, which originated about 1550, first reached a peak of great artistic significance under the Venetian master Merulo. While the earliest toccatas (by Andrea Gabrieli and others) consist of nothing more than sustained chords and interlacing scale passages, Merulo broadened the contents of this form by the introduction of imitative sections, in the order T R T or sometimes T R T R T. (T = toccata style, R = ricercar style.) Moreover the harmonies as well as the passage work of his toccata sections are treated with a boldness and imagination which is a far cry from the dryness and sterility of the early toccatas. ¶ Source: Cl. Merulo, *Toccate, Libro secondo* (1604), p. 15.

154. PASSAMEZZO ANTICO. The passamezzo is the most important dance of the sixteenth century. It appeared shortly before 1550, superseding the basse danse and the pavane. Many of the passamezzi (particularly the earlier ones) are not entirely original compositions, but are elaborate variations on a standard melody which occurs first in Spanish sources under the name of "Guardame las vacas" (see No. 124). In Ammerbach's passamezzo this melody can clearly be distinguished in the soprano, which, after every two measures, proceeds from one of its notes to the next. Giovanni Picchi (who stands at the very close of Renaissance keyboard music) treats the theme in a number of most interesting variations (*parte;* only three of six are given here), retaining only the structural basis and general contours of the original melody. ¶ Sources: (a) N. Ammerbach, *Orgel oder Instrument Tabulatur* (1571); (b) G. Picchi, *Intavolatura di balli d'arpicordo* (1620), new ed. O. Chilesotti, *Biblioteca di raritá musicali,* II, 9.

155. LUCA MARENZIO. Marenzio may be said to hold a position in the development of the Italian madrigal similar to that of Schubert in the development of the symphony—on the border line between "classical" repose (represented by Arcadelt and Palestrina; cf. Nos. 130, 142) and "romantic" emotionalism (represented by Gesualdo, Monteverdi; cf. No. 161). Noteworthy features of the present example are the purely homophonic beginning, the use of a short and characteristic motif for the imitative section "tal che m'avviso," and the clearly contrasting effect of the sustained chords immediately following, in which the idea of "stando in terra" is portrayed. Another example of word painting is the rising scale used at the close for the word "paradiso." ¶ Source: A. Einstein, *Luca Marenzio, Sämtliche Werke,* I (1929), 25.

156. JACOB HANDL. Handl, also known under the Latinized name of Gallus (Handl = *Hahn,* i.e., cock, Latin *gallus*), is the leading German representative of the school of Palestrina. His "Ecce quomodo" is a typical example of sixteenth-century "familiar style," characterized by the abandoning of rhythmic individuality of the voice parts. ¶ Source: *DTOe* XII, 171. ¶ Record: *GSE,* p. 224.

157. GIOVANNI GABRIELI. Giovanni Gabrieli represents the culmination of the Venetian School which was inaugurated by Willaert and included, among others, Andrea Gabrieli and Claudio Merulo. In Gabrieli, the Venetian penchant for magnificent display and splendid pomp came to its fullest realization. With extraordinary boldness and imagination he ventured into entirely new domains of musical expression and structure. His choral writing far exceeds in its brilliant sonorities anything written before his time. "In ecclesiis" is a truly magnificent work for double chorus, solo voices, brass instruments, *violino* (actually a viola, the violin being called at that time violino piccolo), and organ. Obviously this is one of the later works of Gabrieli, incorporating as it does the early Baroque achievements of the *stile concertato,* that is, the combined use of voices and instruments. For the organ, the bass part only is given in the original, in the manner of thorough-bass technique. A full organ accompaniment has therefore been added in small notes. Naturally, in a composition of this period the realization of the thorough-bass has to follow methods entirely different from the familiar methods of the period of Corelli or of Bach. It will be seen that the organ style of Claudio Merulo (see No. 153) has served as a model in the present case. ¶ Source: C. von Winterfeld, *Johannes Gabrieli und sein Zeitalter* (1834), III, 73ff. ¶ Record: *Victor M 928.*

158. GIOVANNI GASTOLDI. In the later part of the sixteenth century there developed various special types of light popular music, such as the villanella, villota, balletto, mascherata, etc. Gastoldi excelled in this field, and became particularly famous for his ballettos, light-hearted little pieces written with an easy hand. Most of them have a "fa-la-la" burden, hence the name Fa-las for such songs. ¶ Source: G. Gastoldi, *Balletti a cinque voci . . .* (1595).

159. THOMAS MORLEY. Gastoldi's style won great acclaim in England, and its influence may be seen from time to time in the work of Thomas Morley. Morley is one of the most characteristically English of the secular composers of the sixteenth century. His music frequently suggests the spirit of English folksong. ¶ Source: Thomas Morley, *The First Book of Ballets to 5 Voices* (1598), new edition by E. H. Fellowes, *The English Madrigal School*, IV, 23.

160. FELICE ANERIO. The present example serves to illustrate the blurring of the borderlines between vocal and instrumental music which took place towards the end of the sixteenth century, foreshadowing the Baroque practice of accompanied song. In the original edition this composition (as well as many other similar ones) is given in three versions, for three-part chorus, for harpsichord, and for lute. Our rendition follows closely the notation of the original source in which the choral version is given on one page, the two others on the next. Needless to say, the vocal and instrumental parts can be combined in various ways, one possibility being the combination of the soprano part with the lute version as an accompaniment, as in the earlier Spanish lute songs (cf. No. 123). ¶ Source: *Ghirlanda di Fioretti Musicali* (1589), p. 29f.

161. CARLO GESUALDO. In the hands of Gesualdo the madrigal became the vehicle of daring experiments and novel thoughts, foreshadowing the basic tendencies of Baroque music. He developed a highly personal style which, although not free from a certain mannerism, is always full of vitality and imagination. He is particularly famous for his daring ventures in the field of harmonies and chromaticism. Another typical trait of his style is the use of short, excited motives which are imitated at a very close distance and which are abruptly abandoned for new motives or contrasting sections in sustained chords. All these traits combine into a picture of utter refinement and nervous instability, creating a fin-de-siècle atmosphere not unlike that of Debussy's impressionism. ¶ Source: C. Gesualdo, *Partitura delli sei libri de' madrigali a cinque voci,* 6th book (1613), fol. 210v.

162. JOHN DANYEL. Among the numerous English masters of the ayre John Danyel takes a prominent place, particularly because of his subtle feeling for textual declamation, illustrated in the present composition. The use of a viola da gamba for the reinforcement of the bass indicates the beginning of a practice which was to become of fundamental importance in the period of Baroque music. Our rendition gives the bar-lines as they appear in the original edition. ¶ Source: John Danyel, *Songs for the Lute Viol and Voice* (1606), no. 7.

163. JOHN DOWLAND. Dowland is the most famous of the lutenist song writers of the Elizabethan period. "Semper dolens" (always grieving), as he said of himself, he was particularly inclined to express in music the sorrows of love and the general spirit of melancholy which were fashionable in the poetry of the time. Lighter tints were not missing on his palette however, as is shown by the present example, with its charming refrain "Come, come." This song is another example of the late sixteenth-century practice of performing the same song in various ways (see No. 160). The original edition shows a peculiar arrangement of the various parts which throws an interesting light on that practice. On the left-hand page of the opened book is printed the soprano part with the lute accompaniment directly underneath, as in a modern accompanied song. The right-hand page shows the parts for the three lower voices arranged in such a manner that they can be read simultaneously by three singers seated north, south, and east of a table. The second stanza of the song is as follows:

> Oft have I dream'd of joy,
> Yet I never felt the sweet,
> But, tired with annoy,
> My griefs each other greet.
> Oft have I left my hope
> As a wretch by fate forlorn;
> But love aims at one scope
> And lost will still return.
> He that once loves with a true desire never can depart,
> For Cupid is the king of every heart.
> Come, while I have a heart to desire thee,
> Come, for either I will love or admire thee.

¶ Source: J. Dowland, *The Third and Last Booke of Songs or Aires* (1603), no. 9.

164. HANS LEO HASSLER: "Quia vidisti me." Hassler is the foremost German composer of the period around 1600. His compositions show the influence of Lassus, or, in many cases, of Giovanni Gabrieli. In his motet "Quia vidisti me" he proves himself a gifted follower of the former master, except for the closing "alleluia" section, which is somewhat monotonous and repetitious. However, such echo effects form a characteristic trait of the period (cf. No. 181). ¶ Source: *DdT* II, 31.

165. HANS LEO HASSLER: "Ach Schatz." As a composer of German secular songs, Hassler stands in direct line of succession to his great predecessors Isaac and Senfl. In

the deep feeling expressed in his compositions there is a quality which is essentially German, and this manifests itself particularly in his melodies. Hassler's secular music is as fundamentally German as Morley's is English. ¶ Source: *DTB* II, 112.

166. GREGOR AICHINGER. Aichinger, side by side with Handl and Hassler (No. 156, No. 164), belongs to that group of musicians who carried on the tradition of Lassus in the various cities of southern Germany, thus helping to lay a foundation for the splendid development of German music in the ensuing centuries. In his motet "Factus est," Aichinger, though making rather too much use of note repetition, nevertheless employs this technique advantageously from the point of view of a clear and forceful delivery of the text. ¶ Source: A. Proske, *Musica divina*, II, 188. ¶ Record: *GSE*, p. 2.

167. MICHAEL PRAETORIUS. Praetorius, though long famous as the author of a highly important theoretical book, the *Syntagma musicum*, did not until much later win due recognition as an outstanding composer of the late Renaissance. Aside from numerous compositions in the established styles and forms of the sixteenth century his complete works contain much of a refreshingly novel character. Most remarkable among these are his elaborations of German chorales, particularly those in two or three parts (*bicinia* and *tricinia*). Their clear and truly polyphonic style offers a delightful contrast to the rich and massive texture which prevails in the choral music of the late sixteenth century. His numerous dance compositions are interesting as early examples of the suite, which was to become of foremost importance in the seventeenth century. ¶ Sources: (a) *Musae Sionae* IX (1610), complete edition by F. Blume (1928ff), IX, 82; (b) *Terpsichore* (1612), complete edition, XV, 160.

168. MELCHIOR FRANCK. Like Hans Leo Hassler (No. 165) Melchior Franck is one of the last masters of the polyphonic German lied. A peculiar feature found in many of his songs is the solo introduction, the initial phrase being sung by the tenor only. Possibly this is a reminiscence of a mastersinger tradition. Another feature suggestive of this relationship is the use of the *Bar* form, a a b (see No. 20). ¶ Source: *Musikalischer Bergreihen* (1602), new edition, *Das Chorwerk*, XXXVIII, 12.

169. THOMAS TOMKINS. Tomkins stands near the close of the great English polyphonic choral tradition, and he displays those particular virtues which made his predecessors outstanding in this field; an unerring sense of what is vocally effective, a strong feeling for what is appropriate from the singer's point of view, and the power to convey through music the subtler shadings in the meaning of the text. His "When David heard" is, no doubt, one of the most impressive among the many outstanding anthems of the period around 1600. The deeply moving story of David's grief at the death of his son has found here a musical expression which fully measures up to the tragic greatness of the Biblical text. ¶ Source: Thomas Tomkins, *Songs of 3. 4. 5. and 6. Parts* (1622), new edition by E. H. Fellowes, *The English Madrigal School*, XVIII, 112.

170. THOMAS WEELKES. In this ballett the trend towards refinement and subtlety, which is noticeable in the development of English as well as Italian secular music, is carried a good deal further than, for instance, in Morley's ballett given as No. 159. Weelkes was a pioneer in the field of chromatic writing, and by his frequent application of the chromatic principle to the melodic line rather than to the chord he achieved effects unusual in his time which were adopted by English composers who followed him. The second stanza of the present example is as follows:

> See see, your mistress bids you cease
> And welcome love with love's increase;
> Diana hath procured your peace.
> Cupid hath sworn
> His bow forlorn
> To break and burn, ere Ladies mourn.
> Fa la la.

¶ Source: T. Weelkes, *Ballets and Madrigals to Five Voices* (1598, 1608), new edition by E. H. Fellowes, *The English Madrigal School*, X, 32. ¶ Record: *Columbia-4166M*.

171, 172. ORLANDO GIBBONS. Gibbons represents the final culmination of English renaissance music. Of a more serious character than most of his fellow musicians, he excelled particularly in the field of sacred music and in compositions for keyboard (see No. 179). His "O Lord, increase my faith" is an example of the full anthem, though on a small scale. "This is the record of John," on the other hand, is a verse anthem, that is, one in which sections for full chorus alternate with others for accompanied solo voice or voices. These two anthems clearly illustrate Gibbons' pivotal position in the history of English music. He looked back to the older choral tradition of which Byrd was the great exponent, and forward to the coming style of the seventeenth century. Organ accompaniment as well as the accompaniment for viols here given is to be found in manuscripts of "This is the record of John." The editors have selected the one for viols because it is more typical of Gibbons' style in accompanimental writing. ¶ Source: *Tudor Church Music*, IV, 270, 297.

173. GIOVANNI GABRIELI: "Sonata pian' e forte." Numbers 173 to 181 serve to illustrate the status of instrumental and keyboard music about 1600. Gabrieli's "Sonata pian' e forte" is one of the most famous products of an extensive activity in this field. It is the earliest extant composition which makes use of the contrast between piano and forte, and Gabrieli apparently thought so much of this innovation as to make it a part of the title of his work. It is written for two groups of instruments, which, if sounding singly, play piano, but repeatedly unite their forces in a pompous forte. Another claim to precedence lies in the fact that this composition is the first to show a detailed indication of the instruments. Therefore it stands at the beginning of the history of orchestration. There is little reason, however, to give it a prominent place in the history of the sonata; its connection with the development of this form is merely nominal. ¶ Source: *Istituzioni e monumenti dell' arte musicale italiana*, II, 64 (1932). ¶ Record: *AS-25* (*GSE*, p. 177).

174. GIOVANNI MACQUE. Macque was a Flemish composer who settled down in Naples where he founded a remarkable school of keyboard music, with Antonio Valente, Giovanni Trabaci, and Ascanio Mayone as his successors. This school forms the link between the organ music of the sixteenth century (particularly Cabezon) and that of Frescobaldi. Macque's "Consonanze stravaganti" (extravagant consonances) is an interesting study in appoggiatura chords and chromatic modulations, an illustration of the same tendencies which found a more convincing expression in the chromatic madrigals of his contemporary Gesualdo (see No. 161). The appoggiatura style of this composition recurs in Frescobaldi's "Toccate di durezza e ligatura." ¶ Source: J. Watelet, *Monumenta Musicae Belgicae* (1932–38), IV, 37.

175. FLORENTIO MASCHERA. Although the history of the instrumental canzona (that is to say, an instrumental piece modeled after the style of the polyphonic vocal chanson) can be traced back as far as the end of the fifteenth century (see Nos. 78, 88), it was not until the late sixteenth century that a continuous development started, a development which was to be of profound consequence, leading, as it did, to the Baroque sonata. Maschera stands at the very beginning of this development, and the canzona reproduced here serves to illustrate its point of departure. The canzona is written in a lively and idiomatically instrumental style, falls into various sections of contrapuntal imitation, but does not show any stylistic contrast between these sections, as does the canzona by Andrea Gabrieli reproduced as No. 136. ¶ Source: *Canzoni di Florentio Maschera, novamente ristampate per i professori d'organo, Libro primo* (1590), p. 29.

176. THOMAS TOMKINS: "In Nomine." The *In Nomine* (also spelt *Innomine*) is exclusively an English type of instrumental music. For more than one hundred years English musicians wrote numerous In Nomines, Taverner being the first and Purcell the last. All these In Nomines are cantus-firmus compositions, based on the same cantus firmus: d f d d d c f g f g a. . . . Why these pieces should have been named "In Nomine" is not clear. The cantus firmus has no relationship to the introit "In nomine Jesu," but is almost identical with the melody of the antiphon "Gloria tibi trinitas." The present example, with its contrast between the sustained bass part and the two quickly moving upper parts, shows a texture strikingly similar to the trio style of the late seventeenth century, exemplified by Lully and Corelli, except for the missing thorough-bass accompaniment. ¶ Source: Transcript from the original, made by Dr. E. B. Helm.

177. JOHN MUNDAY. Munday is a prominent figure among the numerous English keyboard composers of the late sixteenth century known as virginalists, from virginal, the English sixteenth-century name for harpsichord. The large repertory of virginalist literature includes dances (mostly pavanes and galliards, see No. 179), preludes (see No. 178), liturgical organ pieces, fantasias, and variations. In the last-named category particularly, the virginalists made important contributions towards the development of an idiomatic harpsichord style by the introduction of broken-chord figures, rapid passage work, scales in parallel thirds and sixths (occasionally for one hand), etc. In the variations by Munday (also attributed to Morley) on the folk song "Goe from my window," these technical means are used with remarkable taste and ingenuity. Variations No. 3 and No. 6 are here omitted. ¶ Source: *Fitzwilliam Virginal Book*, edited by Fuller Maitland and Barclay Squire, I, 153. ¶ Record: *GSE*, p. 304, where the variations are attributed to Morley.

178. JOHN BULL. Of the "three famous masters William Byrd, Dr. John Bull and Orlando Gibbons" (as they are called in the title of the *Parthenia*, the first printed book of virginal music, published in 1611), John Bull owes his fame to his achievements as a virtuoso rather than as a composer. Many of his compositions are over-extended and rather dull. The present prelude certainly is an exception to this rule, as are also some of his pavanes and galliards. Particularly remarkable is the natural retardation of the motion towards the close of the prelude, leading from the running sixteenth-notes to a passage in dotted rhythm, to eighth-note motion, and to a final measure in quarter notes. ¶ Source: *Fitzwilliam Virginal Book*, edited by Fuller Maitland and Barclay Squire, I, 158.

179. ORLANDO GIBBONS: "Pavane Lord Salisbury." Byrd, Bull, and Gibbons, born at intervals of twenty years (1543, 1563, and 1583 respectively), represent three successive generations in the development of virginal music. Gibbons as an instrumental composer is a typical example of a "late" master whose *fin-de-siècle* personality exudes the fascination of an approaching decadence, but whose creative power is still unbroken. The pavane which he wrote for the Lord of Salisbury is a masterpiece whose utter technical refinement and transcendental spirituality recall the late sonatas of Beethoven. Like many pavanes of the sixteenth century, this composition consists of three sections, each of which develops a different thought (see Nos. 104, 137). Particularly noteworthy is Gibbons' mastery of the musical phrase, which he treats, not in the stereotyped pattern of a four-measure unit, but as a continuous flow carrying the musical thought far beyond its expected limit. ¶ Source: M. H. Glyn, *Orlando Gibbons, Complete Keyboard Works*, vol. III. ¶ Record: *GSE*, p. 180.

180. JEAN TITELOUZE. Our knowledge of the development of keyboard music in France during the sixteenth century is sorely incomplete, owing to the loss of practically all sources between the publications of Attaingnant in 1530 (see No. 104) and the organ works of Titelouze, published in 1623 and 1626. Titelouze's compositions are all liturgical organ pieces of a strongly conservative and somewhat academic character, similar in style to the more inspired works of Cabezon. The "Pange lingua" has the cantus firmus in the lowest part and free contrapuntal lines in the others. ¶ Source: A. Guilmant, *Archives des maîtres d'orgue*, 1, 26.

181. JAN PIETERSZON SWEELINCK: "Fantasia in echo." Sweelinck is by far the most influential of all the organ composers of the late sixteenth century, casting his shadow far ahead into the period of Baroque music. The majority of his pupils came from Germany, which at that time was just emerging as a leading member in the family of musical nations, and he well deserved the title accorded him of "deutscher Organistenmacher" (maker of German organists). He absorbed the figurative harpsichord style of the virginalists as well as the contrapuntal elements of Italian keyboard music, and combined these with many novel traits. Among the latter his extended use of echo effects—illustrated in our example—is particularly worth noticing, all the more so as he treated this somewhat dangerous device with great ingenuity. ¶ Source: Sweelinck, *Complete Works* (edited by M. Seiffert), 1, 51.

TRANSLATIONS

The following translations of the literary texts appearing with the music are quite literal, for the most part, and when it is practicable, are given line for line. For passages from scripture or the liturgy, however, we have used the familiar words of the Authorized Version of the English Bible or the Book of Common Prayer.

2. *Fuki No Kyoku*

The so-called Rich and Noble are like grass. The [truly] Rich and Noble, [endowed with] freedom and virtue, are blessed.

4. *Hindu Chant*

[The opening and closing words of the text, *hā-u* and *ājyadoham*, are a sort of magic formula. *Ājya* means "clarified butter"; this was used as an offering in the service of Agni, the god of fire, who served as a messenger between men and the gods. The main text of the hymn, translated here, begins with *murdha* and ends with *devah*. Cf. R. H. Griffith, *Hymns of the Samaveda* (1907), p. 15, verse 5.]

Hā-u: The head of heaven, the ruler of the earth, Agni Vaisvanara, born in holy Order, the sage sovran, guest of men, was generated by the gods as our vessel fit for their mouth: *Ājyadoham*.

5. *Arabian Popular Song*

[It has not been possible to translate this text, which evidently is corrupt.]

6b. *Verses from the Pentateuch*

Then Moses called for all the elders of Israel, and said unto them, Draw out and take you a lamb according to your families, and kill the passover. And ye shall take a bunch of hyssop, and dip it in the blood that is in the bason, and strike the lintel and the two side posts with the blood that is in the bason; and none of you shall go out at the door of his house until the morning.

Ex. 12:21-22.

6c. *Ledovid boruh*

[A Psalm] of David. Blessed be the Lord my strength, which teacheth my hands to war and my fingers to fight: My goodness and my fortress . . .

Ps. 144:1-2.

7a. *First Delphic Hymn*

A: Hark, ye fair-armed daughters of the loud thundering Zeus who dwell in the deep forests of Helicon! Hasten hither, to praise in song your brother Phoebus, of the golden locks, who high above the rocky dwellings of the two-peaked Parnassus, surrounded by the august daughters of Delphi, betakes himself to the waters of limpid Kastalis, visiting at Delphi the prophetic crag.
B: Lo, the famous Attica, with its great city, which, thanks to the prayer of the arms-bearing Triton, inhabits an unassailable region. On holy altars Hephaestus consumes the thighs of bullocks; together Arabian incense rises toward Olympus. The oboe shrilly sounding brings forth music with varied melodies, and the golden sweet-voiced kithara sounds with hymns.

7b. *Hymn to the Sun*

Father of the bright-eyed Dawn, who dost drive thy rosy chariot with the winged courses of thy steeds, delighting in thy golden hair, over the boundless vault of heaven, shedding thy far-piercing ray and turning over all the earth the far-seeing fount of splendor: thy streams of immortal fire bring forth the lovely day. Before thee the gentle chorus of the stars dance over lord Olympus, ever singing their unrestrained song, rejoicing in the lyre of Phoebus. And before thee the silvery Moon in due season leads the way amid throngs of white kine; and thy mild spirit is glad as it speeds through the richly clad firmament.

7c. *Seikilos' Song*

As long as you live, be cheerful; let nothing grieve you. For life is short, and Time claims its tribute.

8a. *Ode for Christmas*

By miracles the Lord has rescued the people, in that He once made the watery wave of the sea into dry land; and being born of His own free will from the Virgin He has paved for us the way to heaven; whom we praise as being substantially equal to His Father and to mortals.

8b. *Hymn from the Octoechos*

We praise the Redeemer who was born in the flesh of the Virgin. For He was crucified for us, and He arose from the dead on the third day, giving us the great mercy.

9a. *Aeterne rerum conditor*

O eternal author of the universe, who rulest the night and the day, and who createst eternity, alleviate our burden.

9b. *Aeterna Christi munera*

With joyous spirit and dutifully offering our praises, we sing the gifts of the eternal Christ and the victories of the martyrs.

10. *Eructavit*

My heart overfloweth with a good matter.

Ps. 45:1.

11. *Psalm 146 with Antiphon*

Praise ye the Lord. Praise the Lord, O my soul.
While I live will I praise the Lord: I will sing praises unto my God while I have any being.
Put not your trust in princes, nor in the son of man, in whom there is no help.

The Lord preserveth the strangers; he relieveth the fatherless and widow: but the way of the wicked he turneth upside down.

Ps. 146:1–3, 9.

Gloria Patri: Glory be to the Father, and to the Son, and to the Holy Ghost; as it was in the beginning, is now, and ever shall be, world without end. Amen.

Antiphon: While I live will I praise the Lord.

12. *Gradual: Haec Dies*

This is the day which the Lord hath made; we will rejoice and be glad in it. Ps. 118:24.

O give thanks unto the Lord; for he is good: for his mercy endureth forever. Ps. 106:1.

13. *Alleluia: Angelus Domini*

For the angel of the Lord descended from heaven, and came and rolled back the stone [from the door] and sat upon it. Matt. 28:2.

14. *Responsorium: Libera Me*

Deliver me, O Lord, from eternal death, on that awesome day: when the heavens and the earth shall shake, when thou comest to judge the world with fire. I am made to tremble and I fear when the judgment comes, and thy wrath is upon us. That day, day of wrath, of calamity and woe, great day and bitter in truth. Grant them eternal rest, O Lord, and may eternal light shine upon them.

15a. *Kyrie*

I. Lord, have mercy upon us.
II. Christ, have mercy upon us.
III. Lord, have mercy upon us.

15b. *Kyrie-Trope: Omnipotens*

I. (1) Omnipotent Father, Lord creator of all: have mercy upon us.
  (2) Fount and source of good, kindly light eternal: . . .
  (3) May thy mercy save us, O good leader: . . .
II. (1) O Christ, Lord, form, power and wisdom of the Father: have mercy upon us.
  (2) O Christ, splendor of the Father, redeemer of the world astray: . . .
  (3) Let us not disdain thy deeds, O gentle Jesus: . . .
III. (1) Sacred spirit of both, and united love: have mercy upon us.
  (2) Perpetual instigator of life, fount purifying us: . . .
  (3) Highest redeemer of sin, bestower of mercy, take away our offense, fill us with thy holy bounty: . . .

16a. *Christus hunc diem*

(1) Christ grants this day for rejoicing to his assembled loving Christians.
(2) O Christ Jesus, son of God, mediator between our nature and the divine,
  Thou hast visited the places of the earth, a new man flying through the ether.
(3) The angels with their ministrations and the clouds crowd about thee as thou art rising to thy Father;
  But who should wonder that the stars and the angels thus serve thee.
(4) This day thou gavest to earth-born men a new and sweet thing, O Lord, a heavenly hope:
(5) Thou thyself, O Lord, a true man, rising above the starry limits of the kingdom.
(6) How great are the joys that fill thy apostles

(7) To whom thou hast granted that they might perceive thee rising to the skies.
(8) What joyous new ranks meet thee in the heavens
(9) As thou bearest upon thy shoulders a flock for a long time dispersed by the wolves.
(10) This flock, O Christ, good shepherd, deign to guard.

16b. *Victimae paschali laudes*

I. Let Christians dedicate their praises to the Easter victim.
II. The lamb has redeemed the sheep; the innocent Christ has reconciled the sinners with the Father.
  Death and life have fought in wondrous conflict; after death the leader of life, living, reigns.
III. Tell us, O Mary, what thou sawest upon thy way?
  I have seen the sepulchre of the living Christ, and the glory of the rising [Christ],
  The angelic witnesses, the veil and the garments.
  Christ, my hope, has arisen, he goes before his own into Galilee.
IV. We know in truth that Christ has arisen from the dead: be merciful unto us, O victorious king: Amen.

16c. *Jubilemus Salvatori*

I. Let us sing to the Saviour whom the heavenly choirs united praise with joy.
  Peace is announced from on high, the earth is joined to heaven, the church to the angels.
II. The Word is united with the flesh, as was predestined.
  Without carnal sin the Virgin gives birth, the temple of the Lord standing alone throughout the ages.
III. O new and wondrous thing, the fire glows in the ruby, but does not destroy it.
  The heavens let fall the dew, the clouds let fall the rain, the mountains gush forth, the hills flow: the root of Jesse grows.
IV. From the root a flower arises as the Prophet foretold, fulfilling the prophecy.
  The root of Jesse signified King David, the stem the Virgin Mother, the flower the Child.
V. Wondrous is the beauty of the flower, which the plenitude of seven-fold grace commends.
  We are recreated in this flower which invites us by its taste, its smell, and its appearance.
VI. Jesus, immortal child, may this day of thy birth give us peace and joy.
  Flower and fruit of a Virgin, whose perfume is life giving, to thee be praise and glory.

17a. *Song of the Ass*

1. Out from lands of Orient
  Was the ass divinely sent.
  Strong and very fair was he,
  Bearing burdens gallantly.
   Heigh, Sir Ass, oh heigh!

4. Red gold from Arabia,
  Frankincense and, from Sheba,
  Myrrh he brought and, through the door,
  Into the Church he bravely bore.
   Heigh, Sir Ass, oh heigh!

7. Stuffed with grass, yet speak and say
  Amen, ass, with every bray:
  Amen, amen say again:
  Ancient sins hold in disdain.
   Heigh, Sir Ass, oh heigh!
  (Translation by H. C. Greene, in *Speculum* VI, 1931)

17b. *Christo psallat*

(1) The Church sings psalms to Christ:
(2) Gentle mercy.
(3) Let the redeemed daughter of Sion
    (4) Give praises to the King of Glory:
(5) Gentle mercy.
    (6) This day He has destroyed death.

17c. *Beata viscera*

The blessed offspring of the Virgin Mary, concealing the power of the spirit under another garment, has pronounced the peace of God and man. O amazing wonder and new joy, the mother, having borne a child, remains a virgin.

17d. *Sol oritur*

The sun rises in the sky like the dew on fleece (?), and Lucifer [here the text is corrupt]. . . . The divine Child is born from the pure body of the virgin child-bearer.

18a. *Pax in nomine*

1. Peace in the name of the Lord! Marcabru made the words and the song. Hear what he tells: how through His kindness the heavenly Lord has made us a place to purify ourselves, such as there never was except beyond the sea, out there toward Josaphas; and I shall tell you about this one, here.

5. There come, of the lineage of Cain, of the first wicked man, so many who do not honor God. We shall see who will be a true friend to him, for, by virtue of the cleansing place Christ will be one with us; and let us drive out the foul wretches who believe in auguries and fates.   (8 stanzas)

18b. *Be m'an perdut*

Indeed all my friends, there around Ventadorn,
Have lost me since my lady does not love me.
I have no reason ever to return there,
So harsh is she toward me and so ill-humored.*
See why she always appears angry and grim:
Because I find joy and peace in her love!
And this is the only thing over which she may lament or complain.   (2 stanzas)

[* Line 4 is corrupt in our source; for a correct reading see C. Appel, *Die Singweisen des Bernart de Ventadorn*, p. 25.]

18c. *Reis glorios*

(1) Glorious King, true light and clarity,
(2) Almighty God, Lord, if it pleases thee,
(3) Be a faithful help to my companion,
    For I have not seen him since the night came,
    And soon it will be dawn.   (6 stanzas)

18d. *Kalenda maya*

(1) The first of May, neither leaf of beech nor song of bird nor flower of sword lily
(2) Pleases me, lady noble and gay, until I receive a speedy messenger
(3) From your fair self who will tell me
(4) The new delight which love brings me,
(5) And joy; and which draws me toward you, true lady.
(6) And may he die of his wounds, the jealous one, before I take my leave.   (5 stanzas)

19a. *Ja nuns hons pris*

(1) Indeed, no captive can tell his story
    Properly, unless it be sadly.
(2) But with an effort, he can make a song.
    I have many friends, but poor are their gifts.
(3) They will be put to shame, if for ransom
    I am held here for two winters.

19b. *Quant voi*

(1) At the end of the summer when I see the leaves fall
(2) And the great prettiness of the birds come to an end,
(3) Then I feel a desire to sing greater than is my wont.
    For she to whom I give myself loyally has ordered me to sing;
    Therefore I shall: and when my lady pleases, I shall have joy.

19c. *Douce dame*

(1) "Sweet and gentle lady!"
    "Fauvel, what do you wish?"
(2) "I give you my heart without restraint."
    "You are out of your mind."
(3) "Don't you care?" "Out upon you, wretch!"
    "What shall I do now?" "Indeed I shall not give you my love."   (3 stanzas)

19d. *En ma dame*

(1) *In my lady I have placed my heart*
(2) *And my mind.*
(3) I shall not leave her for any reason:
(4) *In my lady I have placed my heart.*
(5) I was overcome by her grey eyes
    (6) Laughing and clear:
(7) *In my lady I have placed my heart*
    (8) *And my mind.*

19e. *Vos n'aler*

(1) *You don't live as I do.*
    (2) *Nor do you know how to live thus.*
        Nor do you know how to live thus.
(3) Fair Alice arose one morning,
(4) *You don't live as I do.*
(5) Dressed herself fairly and decked herself better.
    (6) Good-day to her whom I dare not name;
        Often she makes me sigh.
(7) *You don't live as I do.*
    (8) *Nor do you know how to live thus,*
        Nor do you know how to live thus.

19f. *C'est la fin*

(1) *This is the end, no matter what be said:*
    I shall love.
    (2) It is down there amidst the fields.
    (3) *This is the end, I wish to love.*
(4) Games and dances are being held there,
    A fair friend have I.
(5) *This is the end, no matter what be said:*
    I shall love.

19g. *E, dame jolie*

(1) *Ah, pretty lady,*
    My heart, without deceit,
    I put in your keeping,
    For I do not know your equal.

(2) Often I go complaining
And bemoaning in my heart
Over a discomfort

(3) Which should rejoice
The heart of every lover
Who is overcome by such an ill.

(4) So greatly pleases me
The sweet pain of love,
That I must sing
At its command.

(5) *Ah, pretty lady,*
My heart, without deceit,
I put in your keeping,
For I do not know your equal.

(3 stanzas)

19h. *Pour mon cuer*

(1) To rejoice my heart
I wish to make a song.

(2) I wish to sing to you without argument
Of a very comely lass

(3) Whom I love with all my heart,
May God let it here appear.

(4) Indeed I shall never tire of loving her
For she has captured all my heart in her net.

(5) If the cuckold were to have his arms broken,
I would find more favor with his wife.

19i. *Espris d'ire*

[Owing to the deliberate obscurity of the text, which was a tradition in this form, it has been considered best merely to summarize the contents.]

(A) "Overcome with sorrow and love" the poet bemoans his unsuccessful suit which is driving him to madness. (B) She drives the poet from her company and treats him harshly. But by humiliating himself he increases his honor. (D) He begs the lady to abandon her haughty attitude which does her no credit. (E) If she does not change her attitude, he has no hope save in death. (H) He must either succeed in winning her, or die. (I) He begs Love to change her arrogance to pity: "Thus you will have put life in me instead of death; on such a comforting note I close my descort."

20a. *Swâ eyn vriund*

Whenever one friend stands by another
In full loyalty, without false deed,
There the friend's aid is indeed good.
To him to whom he grants it willingly,
So that they are in complete agreement,
His kin increases in numbers.
Wherever friends are well disposed to each other
Then that is a great joy.

20b. *Nû al'erst*

(1) Now at last my life seems worth while
Now that my sinful eyes behold

(2) Here the land and soil
Which men hold in such high honor.

(3) I have attained that for which
I so often prayed:
I have set foot on the spot
That God in human form has trod.

20c. *Der May*

"May has lifted up many hearts"
Said a young maid. "He has shown
Full well, what his sweet joy can do,
When he clothes the blackthorn in white blossoms.
All that winter had in his time overcome
May now is about to make young again."

20d. *Winder wie ist*

(1) Winter, how has your strength been brought low
Since May has struck you with his spear!

(2) On the meadows before the woods one sees standing in full splendor
Brilliant, beautiful flowers; of these I have plucked

(3) Through a miracle I heard quite plainly:
Men and women, you are all to look upon the meadows
And see how the shining host of May stands clad in royal purple.
Young maids, take heed and do not plight your troth.

21a. *Gloria in cielo*

Glory in heaven and peace on earth! Born is our Saviour. Born is Christ the glorious. The high, miraculous God has made himself a man full of desire, the benign creator.

21b. *A tutta gente*

(1) *To all people I make my prayer and ask*
That they join me in praising the fair Marguerite.

(2) O virgin who, when still young,
Sawest that thou didst belong to God, and he made thee his spouse;

(3) And because of thy generosity
Thou didst not wish to be a flower of the world;

(4) Rather didst thou take the Christian faith
Which drives away vain things and makes one a servant of God.

(5) *To all people I make my prayer and ask*
That they join me in praising the fair Marguerite.

21c. *Santo Lorenzo*

(1) *Saint Laurence, martyr of love,*
To Christ thou wast a great servant.

(2) With humility to the holy Father thou wast obedient.

(3) For this all the human race should always praise thee.

(4) Martyr worthy and valiant,
To the Omnipotent thou art a fragrant flower.

(5) *Saint Laurence, martyr of love,*
To Christ thou wast a great servant.

22a. *A Madre*

[This cantiga tells how Mary saved from being burned the son of a Jew whose father had thrown him into the furnace because he had joined the Christians in school and had taken communion.]

The Mother of Him who saved Daniel from the lions,
Saved from the fire
A little child of Israel.
I. There was a Jew in Bourges
Who knew how to make glass,
And his only son—

For he had no other,
As far as I learned—
Studied among the Christian boys at school,
And that was grievous to his father Samuel.
The Mother of Him who saved Daniel from the lions,
Saved from the fire
A little child of Israel.

XI. Because of this miracle
The Jewish woman believed at once;
And the little boy
Was baptized forthwith. But the father who had done
The evil deed, for his wickedness
Suffered the same death
That he had wished to give his son Abel.
The Mother of Him who saved Daniel from the lions,
Saved from the fire
A little child of Israel. (11 stanzas)

22b. *Mais nos faz*

(1) *Oft indeed does Holy Mary*
Cause her Son to pardon us,
We, who through our folly
Continue to falter and err.
　　(2) For her sake God forgave us Adam's sin of tasting
　　(3) The apple for which we suffered grievous woe.
(4) He entered into hell;
But with so much good will
Did she plead with her Son
That for her sake He went to bring him out.
(5) *Oft indeed does Holy Mary*
Cause her Son to pardon us,
We, who through our folly
Continue to falter and err.

22c. *Aque serven*

(1) *She whom all celestial beings serve*
Well knows the cure of mortal wounds.
　　(2) Of such kind did Saint Mary of Salas
　　(3) Work a great miracle for a poor woman who had
(4) Great trust in her, and served her,
Offering candles before her altar.
(5) *She whom all celestial beings serve*
Well knows the cure of mortal wounds.

24. *Der gülden Ton*

[The short rhyme syllables are omitted.]

(1) Praise God the Father on his throne, who graciously makes known to us His word, the treasure of Grace, in many a place.
(2) Thereby we clearly recognize His will from the Holy Scriptures.
(3) These were hitherto quite obscured by the harmful doctrines of men, that have plunged us into grave doubts. The Lord has decreed this for us since we have embraced the path of human error and poison.

25a. *Nos qui vivimus*

We who live praise the Lord now and in eternity.

25b. *Sit gloria Domini*

Glory be to the Lord, in eternity the Lord will rejoice in his works.

25c. *Rex coeli*

King of heaven, Lord of the wave-sounding sea, of the shining Titan [sun] and of the dark earth, thy humble servants entreat thee, by worshipping thee with pious words as thou hast commanded, to free them from their sundry ills.

25d. *Hymn to Saint Magnus*

O noble, humble Magnus, steadfast martyr, virtuous, useful and venerable leader and praiseworthy protector, guard your subjects burdened by the load of their frail flesh.

26a. *Cunctipotens genitor*

All-powerful father, Lord, creator of all: have mercy upon us.
Christ, Lord, splendor, and wisdom of the Father: have mercy upon us.
Sacred spirit of both, united love: have mercy upon us.

26b. *Ut tuo propitiatus*

By thy intervention, may the propitiating Lord join us, purged of our sins, with the citizens of heaven.

26c. *Alleluia: Angelus Domini*

For the angel of the Lord descended from heaven, and came and rolled back the stone [from the door] and sat upon it.
Matt. 28:2.

27a. *Viderunt Hemanuel*

All the ends of the earth have seen Emanuel, the only-begotten Son of the Father, offered for the fall and for the salvation of Israel, man created in time, word in the beginning, born in the palace of the city which he had founded, the salvation of our God. Be joyful in the Lord, all ye lands. [Cf. Ps. 98:3.]

27b. *Cunctipotens genitor*

All-powerful father, Lord, creator of all: have mercy upon us.
Christ, Lord, form, power, and wisdom of the father: have mercy upon us.
Sacred spirit of both, united love: have mercy upon us.

28a–e. *Benedicamus Domino*

Let us praise the Lord. Thanks be to God.

28f. *Domino fidelium—Domino*

Let the faithful devotion of all the faithful call out in joy and praise to the Lord, through whose grace life is renewed. Let the host of the people redeem from exile the house of their father after the remedying of their guilt. . . . (?)

28g. *Dominator—Ecce—Domino*

Dominator: O Lord God who, born of a Virgin Mother, wast sacrificed for man, cleanse us from sin so that, rejoicing with redoubled praise, we may bless thee without end, O Lord.
Ecce: Behold, the womb of a Virgin brings forth the ministry of Christ miraculously, like a ray of light. That birth removes the sin of the first man. Now without end we sing a hymn to the Lord.

28h. *Pucelete—Je languis—Domino*

Pucelete: Fair maid and pleasing pretty one, polite and pleasant, the delightful one whom I desire so much makes me joyous, gay and loving. In May there is no nightingale so gaily singing

I shall love with all my heart my sweetheart who is such a fair brunette. Sweetheart, who have held my life in your command so long, I cry mercy, sighing.

Je languis: I languish from the malady of love. Far rather would I that this illness kill me than any other. [Such] death is very pleasing. Relieve me, sweet friend, of this malady lest love kill me.

28i. II. *Candida Virginitas—Flos Filius*

Candida: The virginity is white like the lily, fecundity is white [pure] through the Son. May the humble exult in joy. Chastity destroys the head of the enemy [text corrupt] . . . through it faith and hope and charity.

Flos filius eius: Her Son is the flower.

III. *Quant revient—L'autre jor—Flos Filius*

Quant revient: When leaves and flowers return with the sweetness of spring, God then reminds me of love, who has ever been courtly and gentle with me, by his help assuaging my pain when I wish. Much wealth and honor comes from following his command.

L'autre jor: The other day I went along a path. I entered a garden to pick flowers. There I found a lady, tastefully dressed, whose heart was gay. There she sang most heartily. I am in love, what shall I do? *This is the end, no matter what be said: I shall love.* [Cf. No. 19f.]

29–31. *Hec dies*

This is the day which the Lord hath made; we will rejoice and be glad in it. Ps. 118:24.

O give thanks unto the Lord, for he is good: for his mercy endureth forever. Ps. 106:1.

32a. *Huic main—Hec dies*

Huic main: This morning in the sweet month of May, as the sun was rising I entered an orchard. Beneath a verdant pine a maid I found, roses picking. Then I drew near her and offered her true love. She replied to me: *Never shall you touch me, for I have a sweet friend.*

32b. *O mitissima (Quant voi)—Virgo—Hec dies*

O mitissima: O sweetest Virgin Mary: beg thy son to give us help and resources against the deceiving tricks of the demons and their iniquities.

Quant voi: When I see returning the summer season, and all the little birds make the wood resound, then I weep and sigh for the great desire which I feel for fair Marion, who has imprisoned my heart.

Virgo: Virgin of virgins, light of lights, reformatrice of men, who bore the Lord: through thee, O Mary, let grace be given, as the angel announced: Thou art a Virgin before and after.

32c. *Deo confitemini—Domino*

Acknowledge the Lord who by His clemency united the flesh with His spirit in Mary, so that He might bring the promised help to the seed of Abraham, conforming himself to man. Thus by his pious death He redeemed [mankind], subject to crime, misled by the enemy's wickedness.

32d. *Trop sovent—Brunete—In seculum*

Trop sovent: Too often do I lament and grieve, and all for her whom I have loved so much, because of her great pride and her haughtiness. *In my lady have I placed my heart and my mind.* [Cf. No. 19d.]

Brunete: Brunete, to whom I have given my love, for you I have endured many grievous ills. In God's name, take pity on me, noble loving heart. *From kindliness comes love.*

33a. *Alle, psallite—Alleluya*

[This text is a trope of the word *Alle- luya.*]

Alle- praise with *luya.* . . . *Alle-* with a full and devoted heart praise God with *luya.*

33b. *On parole—A Paris—Frèse nouvele*

On parole: They speak of beating and winnowing and of digging and of plowing, but these pastimes displease me. For there is no life so good as being at ease, with good clear wine and capons, and to be with good companions, gay and joyous, singing, cheating, and amorous; and to have, when one needs them, fair ladies to solace us as we wish: and all this one finds at Paris.

A Paris: In Paris, morning and night, one finds good bread and good clear wine, good meat and good fish, companions of all sorts, clever wit, great joy, ladies of honor; and also there are, at good occasion, means to live for poverty-stricken men.

Frèse: Fresh strawberries, wild blackberries!

34. *Aucun—Lonc tans—Annuntiantes*

Aucun: Some invent their songs through habit, but it is love which gives me my incentive, rejoicing my heart so that I must make a song. For a lady makes me love her, a lady fair and wise, of good report. And I, who have sworn to serve her all my life with loyal heart and no betraying, I shall sing, for I receive from her so sweet a gift that in it alone I find joy: This is the thought that assuages my sweet ill and makes me hope for cure. Nevertheless love may claim lordship over me and hold me all my life in his prison. Nor indeed shall I blame him for this imprisonment. So subtly does he attack that one cannot defend one's self against him. A strong heart and noble lineage are of no avail. And if he wishes a ransom, I surrender to him and give him as pledge my heart, which I abandon wholly to him. And I beg mercy of him for I have no other resource nor any other reason in my favor.

Lonc tans: For a long time I have refrained from singing, but now I have reason to be joyous, for true love makes me long for the best-bred [lady] whom one can find in all the world. And since I love so priceless a lady, and take so much pleasure in the thought, I can indeed prove that he who loves truly leads a most delicious life, whatever may be said.

35. *Je cuidoie—Se j'ai—Solem*

Je cuidoie: Indeed I thought I had abandoned the sweet occupation of love, but I felt myself more than ever sweetly surprised by a new love for the gracious one whose name is Sweet One, if she be rightly named. She is so sweet in truth that I think very certainly that God and Nature called in Love to form such a creature; for in her there is nothing lacking that she be perfect for love. She is a brunette, wise, knowing, young, slim, savory, and more than any other, pretty. She has a mouth with a sweet red smile, pleasingly; unaffected in her manner is she, and of fair mien; her sweet bright face shows that she is gracious: this makes me most joyfully hope for her favor soon. And I love her so well, Sweet Lord, that I gladly seize the occasion to say: if I have loved too foolishly other than her, I repent of it. And most willingly do I thank Love that after great pain for my folly she gives me great sweetness.

Se j'ai: If I have loved foolishly and most deeply hurt myself without redress, this my heart knows, and feels it. Dearly have I bought it. But now I am glad to be overcome by a love which gives all good; and therefore I repent of having loved so very foolishly.

36a.   *Li maus d'amer*

The pain of love pleases me more
Than do the joys [of love] many a lover,
For my hope is worth as much as another's enjoyment.
Therefore whatever love sends me pleases me well
For the more I suffer, the more it pleases me that I be
Happy and singing.
Therefore I am as gay and as joyous
As if I were more favored.

36b.   *Tant con je vivrai*

(1) *As long as I live*
    (2) *I shall not love another than you.*
(3) I shall not leave
(4) *As long as I live.*
(5) Rather I shall serve you
    (6) Loyally I have given myself wholly to you.
(7) *As long as I live*
    (8) *I shall not love another than you.*

36c.   *Diex soit*

[This is a *chanson de quête*, sung by children at Christmas time for alms.]

(1) *May God dwell in this house*
    And may there be wealth and joy a-plenty.
(2) Our Lord's birth
    Sends us to his friends
      That is to the lovers,
    To the well-bred, courtly ones,
    To get alms
      At Noel.
(3) *May God dwell in this house*
    And may there be wealth and joy a-plenty.
(4) Our Lord is such
    That he [himself] would beg untiringly
      But in his stead to the wicked
    He has sent us
    Whom he has nourished
      And who are his children.
(5) *May God dwell in this house*
    And may there be wealth and joy a-plenty.

37.   *Rex virginum*

I. (1) King, lover of virgins, God, glory of Mary: have mercy upon us.
  (2) Who brought forth Mary from royal stock: . . .
  (3) Receive her prayer, a worthy offering on behalf of the world: . . .
II. (1) Oh Christ, God from the Father, born a man from thy mother, Mary: have mercy upon us.
  (2) Whom Mary gave forth to the world from her holy womb: . . .
  (3) Accept our praises, consecrated to thy beloved Mary: . . .
III. (1) Oh Comforter, protecting the body of Mary: have mercy upon us.
  (2) Who made the body of Mary a worthy chamber: . . .
  (3) Who raisest the spirit of Mary above the skies, Make us ascend after her through thy power, beloved Spirit: . . .

38.   *Roma gaudens jubila*

Let Rome, rejoicing in exultation, today drive the clouds far away; a splendor of the mind, a splendor of peace, glory unto the faithful, sprung from your Lord. Therefore arise from thy sad-

ness, O daughter of Sion! The Lord of Salvation is at hand, so that thine exile may be ended with joy: receive the King of Kings.

39.   *Hac in anni janua*

At this beginning of the year, in this month of January, let us turn to our heavy tasks, assisted by our virtues. The joys are mutual, vice has been made mute. The misguided activities of the evildoers are reproved.

43.   *Detractor est*

Detractor est: A disparager is the most worthless fox. By his slanders he harms others and himself worse. But no less is he a bland flatterer. For he deceives kings, princes, counts, dukes. Such ones are to be fled by all . . . [The remainder of the text is corrupt and, in many places, meaningless; it seems to continue much in the same vein.]

Qui secuntur: Those who follow the camps are wretched, for poorly are their services rewarded . . . [The remainder of the text is corrupt.]

44.   *S'il estoit nulz*

S'il estoit: If there is anyone who should complain of harm received from love, I should indeed complain without restraint. For when love first came to enamor me, what boldness I had would never let me tell of my sadness; rather she took away from me what most made me rejoice and gave me hope of success: looking at her, without saying or doing more. Then she put me in prison, where I had my share of ardent desires which were so displeasing that I more than anyone have a right to say that in truth I cannot live without the help of my gentle lady: she gave me respite, so that I did not have to die. And this is quite proper, for sweet pity and courtliness have their abode in her.

S'amours: If love were to make every lover rejoice at the beginning, he would lessen his worth, for no lover would have the great pleasure that one enjoys in serving a lady of honor. But he who lives in desire, and whom true love perceives, has more pleasures than he could wish for, when joy rewards him. And for this reason, one should feel no regret at loving well, even though his love makes him languish very much. [This text represents a dialectic commentary on the theme of the other text.]

45.   *Je puis trop bien*

(1) I can all too well compare my lady
    To the image which Pygmalion made.
(2) It was of ivory, so beautiful, without peer,
    That he loved it more than Jason did Medea.
(3) Out of his senses, he prayed to it unceasingly,
    But the image answered him not.
    Thus does she treat me who makes my heart melt,
    For I pray her ever, and she answers me not.
                    (3 stanzas)

46a.   *Comment qu'a moy*

(1) *Although you are far from me, my noble lady,*
    Still you are near to me in thought, night and day.
    (2) For memory so leads me that always without respite
    (3) Your sovereign beauty, your gracious appearance,
(4) Your sure manner and your fresh color—
    Neither pale nor ruddy—I see always without respite.
(5) *Although you are far from me, my noble lady,*
    Still you are near to me in thought, night and day.
                    (3 stanzas)

46b. *Plus dure*

(1) *Harder than a diamond*
Or a lodestone
Is your harshness,
Lady, who feel no pity
For your lover whom you kill
As he desires your friendship.

    (2) Lady, your pure beauty,
        Which surpasses all—so I feel—
        And your appearance,

    (3) Simple and modest,
        Bedecked with fine sweetness,
        Smiling,

(4) And with an attractive welcome
Have wounded me so deeply in the heart
    As I looked at you
That never shall I have joy
Until you shall have given me
    Your grace.

(5) *Harder than a diamond*
Or a lodestone
    Is your harshness,
Lady, who feel no pity
For your lover whom you kill
As he desires your friendship.   (3 stanzas)

47. *En attendant*

(1) While waiting, hope comforts
The man who desires fulfillment;

(2) While waiting, he enjoys and disports himself
While waiting for a first reward.

(3) While waiting, time and season passes,
While waiting, he puts his trust in it;
Of all these viands is served in plenty
The one who cannot live without hope.

48a. *Amans ames*

(1) *Lovers, love secretly*
    (2) *If you wish to love long.*
(3) Receive this advice:
(4) *Lovers, love secretly;*
(5) Because whoever does differently
    (6) Makes the sweetness of love bitter.
(7) *Lovers, love secretly,*
    (8) *If you wish to love long.*

48b. *Belle bonne*

(1) *Fair [lady], good, wise, pleasing and noble,*
On this day when the year is renewed
    (2) *I make you a gift of a new song*
    Within my heart which gives itself to you.
(3) Do not be slow to accept this gift,
I beg you, my sweet damsel,
(4) *Fair [lady], good, wise, pleasing and noble,*
On this day when the year is renewed;
(5) Because I love you so much that otherwise I will have no peace,
And indeed I know that you are the only one
    (6) Whose fame is such that all call you:
    Flower of beauty, above all other excelling.

(7) *Fair [lady], good, wise, pleasing and noble,*
On this day when the year is renewed
    (8) *I make you a gift of a new song*
    Within my heart which gives itself to you.

49. *Non al suo amante*

(1) Not did Diana ever please her lover
So much, when through such good fortune he saw her naked
In the midst of the cool waters,

(2) As [pleases] me the rustic and cruel shepherdess
Washing her white veil
Which shall protect her fair hair from the sun and the breeze:

(3) So that it made me, now when the sky is fiery,
All tremble with a chill of love.
    [Cf. Petrarch, ed. Carducci-Ferrari, Madrigal no. 52.]

50. *Nel mezzo*

(1) In the midst of six peacocks, I saw a white one
With crest of gold and soft feathers,
So beautiful that he stole my heart.

(2) And when he shows his beauty
All those of other colors pay him honor
For the graceful appearance of love that he has.

(3) But his companion goes ever looking at him,
And ever singing never parts from him;
And he artfully makes her go from him

    (4) Because her wearisome song displeases him:

    (5) Then for beauty's sake he spreads his tail as a fan and
    cloak.

51. *Io son un pellegrin*

(1) *I am a pilgrim who goes seeking alms,*
Crying mercy for God's sake.
    (2) And I go singing with fine voice,
    With sweet appearance and with blond tresses.
    (3) I have nothing but the pilgrim's staff and wallet,
    And I cry out and cry out and there is no one who
    answers.
(4) And when I am hoping for fair weather,
A contrary wind arises against me.
(5) *I am a pilgrim who goes seeking alms,*
Crying mercy for God's sake.

52. *Tosto che l'alba*

As soon as the dawn of the fair day appears, the hunter awakens. "Arise, arise, for it is now time!" "Call out the dogs; here, here, Viola here, Primera here!" Upon the high mountain with good dogs in hand and the pack silent, and on the long slope each in order. "I see one of our best hounds sniffing. He must be on the trail of something. Let each one of you pierce through, from all sides into the thickets, for the quail calls." "Hola, hola, the hind is coming to you. Carbona has seized her and holds her in his mouth." From the mountain, he who was up there called out now to one, now to another, and sounded his horn.

53. *Amor c'al tuo suggetto*

(1) *Love that now dost give strength to thy subject,*
I live without suffering under thy yoke.
    (2) And thus do I wish to remain forever happy,
    Since thou hast made me a slave to this goddess.

(3) For she cannot be compared to anything,
Such the one who could do everything brought her
forth,

(4) Because every virtue is created in her:
O happy the one whom thou dost bind with such chains.

(5) *Love that now dost give strength to thy subject,*
I live without suffering under thy yoke.

54.   *Sy dolce non sono*

(1) So sweetly did not Orpheus sound with his lyre,
When he drew toward himself beasts, birds, and woods,
Singing of the divine child of Love,

(2) As did my rooster from out the woods,
With such sound as was never heard
From Philomel in the green woods;

(3) Nor more did Phoebus sing when his flute was scorned
By Marsias in the verdant woods,
Where victorious he deprived him of his life.

[The text of the ritornello is corrupt. Apparently it contains an allu-
sion to Amphion, who moved the stones with the music of his lyre, and
the Gorgon, who turned the beholder into stone; hence, Amphion
"facto fa contrario al Gorgone."]

55.   *Et in terra pax*

[Glory be to God on high,] and on earth peace, good will
towards men. We praise thee, we bless thee, we worship thee,
we glorify thee, we give thanks to thee for thy great glory, O Lord
God, heavenly King, God the Father Almighty.

O Lord, the only-begotten Son, Jesus Christ; O Lord God, Lamb
of God, Son of the Father, that takest away the sins of the world,
have mercy upon us. Thou that takest away the sins of the world,
receive our prayer. Thou that sittest at the right hand of God the
Father, have mercy upon us.

For thou only art holy; thou only art the Lord; thou only,
O Christ, with the Holy Ghost, art most high in the glory of God
the Father.

56.   *Credo*

[I believe in one God] the Father Almighty, Maker of heaven
and earth, and of all things visible and invisible: and in one Lord
Jesus Christ, the only-begotten Son of God; begotten of his Father
before all worlds, God of God, Light of Light, Very God of very
God; begotten not made; being of one substance with the Father;
by whom all things were made: who for us men and for our
salvation came down from heaven, and was incarnate by the Holy
Ghost of the Virgin Mary, and was made man.

57a.   *Alleluia psallat*

This congregation sings Alleluia, with cymbals and zithers the
joyous crowd in harmony sings to God praise and glory.

57b.   *Gloria in excelsis*

[Glory be to God on high,] and on earth peace, good will
towards men. We praise thee, we bless thee, we worship thee, we
glorify thee, we give thanks to thee for thy great glory, O Lord
God, heavenly King, God the Father Almighty. O Lord, the only-
begotten Son, Jesus Christ; O Lord God, Lamb of God, Son of
the Father.

60.   *Der May*

May with its charming host
covers all the land,
hill and plain, mountain and vale

resound with sweet bird call;
dove and lark, thrush and nightingale
sing lusty songs.
The cuckoo comes aflying after them,
a terror to the little birds.
Listen to what he says:
cu, cu, cu, cu, cu, cu,
pay me my due,
I must have that from you.
Hunger makes my stomach almost ravenous.
Alack a day! You would
that I should? so spoke the small birds.
Küngel, siskin, titmouse, lark, now we come a-singing:
oci and toowee, toowee, toowee, toowee
Oci . . .
fi . . .
ci . . .
ci ri . . .
And all the while the cuckoo sang only: . . .
Caw, said the crow,
Indeed I sing well too
but I must be full;
my song goes thus:
Shovel it in! all in! must be full!
Liri . . .
so sang the lark, so sang the lark, so sang the lark.
I the little thrush sing clearly, I . . .
That song resounds in the forest.
You pipe you preen yourselves,
you rock and wave
to and fro
just like our priest.
Cidiwigg . . .
Nightingale, she with her song lightened our woe.

61.   *O rosa bella*

O beautiful rose, O my sweet soul, do not let me die in court-
liness. Ah, woe is me, must I end sorrowing for having served
well and loyally loved?

62.   *Sancta Maria*

Holy Mary, in this world there has arisen none like thee among
women. Blooming like the rose, fragrant as the lily, pray for us,
holy Mother of God.

63.   *Sanctus* and *Benedictus qui venit*

Holy, holy, holy Lord God of hosts; heaven and earth are full
of thy glory. Hosanna in the highest.   [Cf. Isaiah 6:3]
Blessed is he that cometh in the name of the Lord. Hosanna in
the highest.   Matt. 21:9.

64.   *Beata Dei genitrix*

Blessed Mary, mother of God, eternal virgin, temple of the Lord,
sanctuary of the Holy Spirit: Thou alone, without example, hast
pleased the Lord Jesus Christ. Pray for the people, intervene for
the clerus, intercede for the devoted feminine sex. Alleluia.

65.   *Alma redemptoris mater*

Gracious Mother of the Redeemer, who stayest at the doors of
heaven, Star of the sea: aid the falling, rescue the people who
struggle. Thou who, to the astonishment of nature, hast borne
thy Creator: Virgin before and after, who heard the *Ave* from
the mouth of Gabriel, be merciful to sinners.

66. *Missa L'Homme armé*

L'homme armé: One must be on guard against the soldier. Everywhere it has been announced that everybody should arm himself with an iron hauberk.

Kyrie: Lord, have mercy upon us.

Agnus Dei: O Lamb of God, who takest away the sins of the world, grant us thy peace.

67. *Mon chier amy*

(1) My dear friend, what is on your mind,
That you indulge in this melancholy,

(2) Though God has been a good friend to you
And has kept you company?

(3) Don't despair of life;
Prithee, give up this grief,
For once we must take this step.   (2 stanzas)

68. *Adieu, m'amour*

Good-by, my love, good-by, my joy
Good-by, what was my solace.
Good-by, my loyal mistress.
To say good-by hurts me so much
That it seems to me that I must die.

69. *De plus en plus*

(1) *More and more there is renewed,*
My sweet lady, noble and fair,
My will to see you.

(2) *Hence comes my very great desire*
To hear news of you.

(3) Don't think that I hold back,
Since always you are the one
Whom I wish to obey.

(4) *More and more there is renewed,*
My sweet lady, noble and fair,
My will to see you.

(5) Alas, if you are cruel to me
I shall have such anguish in my heart
That I shall want to die:

(6) But this would be without abandoning your service
And still upholding your cause.

(7) *More and more there is renewed,*
My sweet lady, noble and fair,
My will to see you.

(8) *Hence comes my very great desire*
To hear news of you.

70. *Files à marier*

Girls to be married, never marry. For if there be jealousy, never will you or he have joy in your heart.

71. *Puisque je voy*

(1) Since I see, my pretty one, that you do not love me
And that you have chosen some one else,

(2) My heart, indeed, is so wounded
That all pleasure has left it.

(3) Alas, ah me, my deeds are all evil
And hence I have nothing but sorrow and cares!

(4) Since I see, my pretty one, that you do not love me
And that you have chosen some one else,

(5) Nevertheless, I am sure that when you have considered well
That I am yours and that I have served you

(6) You will realize that you were wrong
And that you had no reason to act thus.

(7) Since I see, my pretty one, that you do not love me
And that you have chosen some one else,

(8) My heart, indeed, is so wounded
That all pleasure has left it.

72. *Ce ieusse fait*

If I had done what I am thinking
And if I were in my country,
I would be more than satisfied
To see such an outcome.

73a. *Kyrie*

Lord, have mercy upon us.
Christ, have mercy upon us.
Lord, have mercy upon us.

73b. *Agnus Dei*

O Lamb of God, who takest away the sins of the world: grant us thy peace.

74. *Ma maîtresse*

(1) *My mistress and my greatest friend,*
The mortal enemy of my desire,
Perfect in qualities if ever woman was;
She whom, alone, fame and rumor report
As being without peer, shall I never see you?

(2) Alas, I should indeed complain of you,
If it does not please you to let me see you again shortly,
My love, who make me unable to love another.

(3) For without seeing you wherever I am,
Everything that I see displeases and angers me,
Nor shall I be satisfied until then.

(4) Endlessly my sorrowing heart weeps,
Fearing lest your pity have fallen asleep.
May this never be, my well-beloved lady,
But if it is true, I am so unhappy
That I do not wish to love an hour longer, nor even a half.

(5) *My mistress and my greatest friend,*
The mortal enemy of my desire,
Perfect in qualities if ever woman was;
She whom, alone, fame and rumor report
As being without peer, shall I never see you?

75. *Ma bouche rit*

(1) *My mouth laughs and my heart weeps.*
My eye rejoices and my heart curses the hour
When it received that good which destroys my health,
And that pleasure with which death pursues me
Without consolation to aid or succor me.

(2) Ah, perverse, lying, and deceiving heart,
Tell me how you have dared to think
Of not fulfilling what you have promised me.

(3) Since you wish to avenge yourself this much,
You should know that you are cutting short my life.
I cannot live thus as you have made me.

(4) Your pity demands then that I die,
But my fate demands that I remain alive.

Thus I die living, and living pass away,
Only to hide the pain which does not cease
And to cover the grief under which I labor.

(5) *My mouth laughs and my heart weeps.*
My eye rejoices and my heart curses the hour
When it received that good which destroys my health,
And that pleasure with which death pursues me
Without consolation to aid or succor me.

76a. *O beate Basili*

O blessed Basil, venerable confessor of the Lord, by the merits of whose life a column of fire lit from on high hath appeared, pray to Christ for thy servants that He may forgive us, his friends.
O blessed Father Basil, implore the Lord Jesus for our impieties.

76b. *O vos omnes*

All ye that pass by, behold and see if there be any sorrow like unto my sorrow.   Lamentations I:12.

77a. *Kyrie I*

Lord, have mercy upon us.

77b. *Agnus Dei II*

O Lamb of God, who takest away the sins of the world: have mercy upon us.

79. *Royne du ciel*

Queen of heaven, who with virginal milk
Hath moistened the face of the Son of God,
Save me from lodgings of hell,
For thou art the treasurer of grace.

80. *Veni sancte spiritus—Veni creator spiritus*

Come, Holy Spirit, and send forth the ray of thy light from heaven.
Come, creating Spirit, visit the minds of thine own, fill with thy high grace the hearts which thou hast created.

81. *Mit ganczem Willen*

Since I have surrendered myself to you
With all my soul I wish you well.
If it is your wish
Then I will place myself
Completely in your command,
My lady dear, 't is true.
Thus I will be yours alone,
My dearest lady.

82. *Quodlibet: O rosa bella*

O beautiful rose, O my sweet soul, do not let me die in court-liness. Oh, woe is me, must I end sorrowing for having served well and loyally loved?   [Cf. No. 61.]
[*Snatches of German songs*]
1. In fire's heat my heart burns.
2. My tender love.
3. It troubles me.
4. Help and advise.
5. Be joyous.
6. Look into my heart.
7. My dear companion.
8. May is gone.
9. Desirable fair one.
10. Success, cash and luck, heart full of lust.
11. I saw once.
12. My only hope.

13. God bless you.
14. Thus, my dear beloved.
15. I never knew what real love was.
16. I am forgotten.
17. O force of desire.
18. Friendly place, what (?)
19. If I love, I suffer.
20. Open, my dearest love.
21. At all times.
22. I take my leave, and that must be.

87. *Zwischen Berg und tiefem Tal*

Between the mountain and the deep valley
There runs a free highroad.
Whoever does not wish to keep his love,
Must let him go.

89. *Agnus Dei*

O Lamb of God, who takest away the sins of the world: have mercy upon us.

90. *Tu pauperum refugium*

Thou art the refuge of the poor, alleviator of weakness, hope of the exiled, strength of the heavy-laden, path for the erring, truth and life. And now, Lord redeemer, I take refuge in thee alone; I worship thee, the true God. In thee I hope, in thee I trust. My salvation, Jesus Christ, uphold me, in order that my soul may never sleep in death.

91. *Faulte d'argent*

Lack of money is an evil without equal. If I say so, alas, I know well why! Without the wherewithal one must keep very quiet. [But] a woman that sleeps wakes up for cash.

92. *Kyrie*

Lord, have mercy upon us.

93. *Mein's traurens ist*

(1) There is good reason for my plaint.
My grief is
That I may voice my grief
(2) To no one but to you,
My shining sun.
On your account I suffer pain.
(3) I would, believe me,
Sooner choose death
Than lose you.

94. *Ave Maria*

Hail Mary, full of grace, the Lord is with thee; blessed art thou among women, and blessed is the offspring of thy womb, Jesus. Holy Mary, Mother of God, pray for us sinners, now and in the hour of our death. Amen.

95a. *Non val aqua*

(1) *Water avails not for my great fire,*
Which is not quenched by tears.
    (2) *On the contrary, it increases*
    Ever more the more I weep.
(3) *My fire has [become] such a habit*
That it even increases by tears,

(4) And takes on greater power
When my purpose does not succeed.

(5) And my fire is like the fish
Which has its proper place in the water.

(6) *Water avails not for my great fire,*
Which is not quenched by tears. (6 stanzas)

95b. *In te Domine*

(1) *In Thee, Lord, did I put my hope*
To find pity for ever;

(2) But in a sad and dark Hell
Was I and suffered in vain.

(3) Broken and [scattered] to the wind [is] my hope;
I see Heaven turn me to weeping;

(4) Sighs, tears remain to me
Of my sad hope [once] so great.

(5) I was hurt; however
In my sorrow I called to Thee.

(6) *In Thee, Lord, did I put my hope*
To find pity for ever. (4 stanzas)

96. *Per scriptores*

Come, come, fair sirs,
Whoever wishes to dispatch his bulls,
Let him come to us who are scribes.
Come, sirs, if you wish
To turn out your bulls,
And will send them to us,
We will not make you wait long for them,
But are willing to make an agreement
To turn out as many as
Eight per day, and do as good a job
As any other scribe.

[The text is a satirical comment on the notoriously slow redaction of papal bulls.]

97a. *Oh dulce*

O, sweet, sad memory!
O the pain with the bliss
Of that past glory
In which I once rejoiced! (2 stanzas)

97b. *Durandarte, Durandarte*

Durandarte, Durandarte,
Knight doughty and true,
Let us speak, I prithee,
Of time gone by (5½ stanzas)

98a. *Congoxa mas que cruel*

(1) An anguish worse than cruel
My saddened life combats,
The cause was my departure.

(2) To depart, yet not relinquish

(3) The thought of you, gracious and gentle lady,

(4) So saddens my life
That better it will be to die.
The cause was my departure. (4 stanzas)

98b. *Pues que jamas olvidaros*

(1) Since now my heart
Can ne'er forget you,
Should it lack reward,
Ah, the wrong I did to gaze upon you!

(2) That vision of you will bring
Sadness and sorrow;

(3) Only pain can that vision be,
Should fortune fail me:

(4) But if you, for my true love,
Will but reward me,
Then my heart will never say,
Ah, the wrong I did to love you! (3 stanzas)

98c. *Mas vale trocar*

(1) Better exchange
Pleasure for grief
Than live without love.

(2) Where it is honored
To die is sweet;

(3) To live forgotten
Is not to live;

(4) Better to suffer
Passion and grief
Than live without love. (4 stanzas)

106. *Agnus Dei*

O Lamb of God, who takest away the sins of the world: have mercy upon us.
O Lamb of God, who takest away the sins of the world; have mercy upon us.
O Lamb of God, who takest away the sins of the world: grant us thy peace.

107. *L'Alouette*

[Much of this text consists of nonsense words piled up in the style of Rabelais. There follows a translation of selected portions of the text.]

Or sus: Get up, get up, you sleep too much, my pretty lady, the day is here, arise! Listen to the lark.

Qu'on tue: Let this false rival be killed, the horned cuckold, all awry, misshapen, he is not worth the trousers of an old hanged man.

Qu'il soit: Let him be tied, bound, shut up, beaten, and thrown into a ditch. Or let him suffer in some other manner. When one offers to kiss his wife, to embrace her, to knock her over, let every one do as he pleases, or else go off and die.

108. *Christ ist erstanden*

Christ has arisen from all His sufferings. Therefore we shall all rejoice, Christ will be our consolation. Kyrieleison.

109. *Salutatio prima*

Hail, O Lord Jesus Christ, blessed king, word of the Father, son of the Virgin, Lamb of God, salvation of the world, sacred host, word made flesh, fountain of mercy.

110. *Da Jakob nu das Kleid ansah*

When Jacob now saw the coat,
He spake with great dolor:
Ah, the great woe,
My dear son is dead.
The evil beasts have devoured him,
And have rent his coat with their teeth.
Oh Joseph, my dear son!
Who shall now console me in my old age?
For I must die of grief,
And sadly go from this earth.

111.

Aus tiefer Not

[This is a rhymed paraphrase of Ps. 130:1–3.]

Out of the depths have I cried unto thee, O Lord.
Lord, hear my voice: let thine ears be attentive to the voice of my supplications.
If thou, Lord, shouldest mark iniquities, O Lord, who shall stand?

112.

Benedictus

Blessed [is he] who cometh in the name of the Lord. Hosannah in the highest.

113.

Victimae paschali laudes

Let Christians dedicate their praises to the Easter victim.
The lamb has redeemed the sheep; the innocent Christ has reconciled the sinners with the Father. Death and life have fought in wondrous conflict; after death the leader of life, living, reigns.

114.

Super flumina

By the rivers of Babylon, there we sat down, yea, we wept, when we remembered Zion.
We hanged our harps upon the willows in the midst thereof.
For there they that carried us away captive required of us a song; and they that wasted us required of us mirth, saying, Sing us one of the songs of Zion.
How shall we sing the Lord's song in a strange land?
Ps. 137:1–4.

123.

Paseábase el rey

The Moorish king was walking
Through the city of Granada.
Letters had come to him
How Alhama had been taken.
Alas! my Alhama!

125.

Vox in Rama

In Rama was there a voice heard, lamentation, and weeping, and great mourning, Rachel weeping for her children, and would not be comforted, because they are not. Matt. 2:18.

126.

Deba contre mes debateurs

[This is a rhymed paraphrase of Ps. 35:1–3.]

Plead my cause, O Lord, with them that strive with me: fight against them that fight against me.
Take hold of shield and buckler, and stand up for mine help.
Draw out also the spear, and stop the way against them that persecute me: say unto my soul, I am thy salvation.

127.

Audivi vocem

I heard a voice coming from heaven: Take oil in your vessels, while the bridegroom tarries. And at midnight there was a cry made, Behold, the bridegroom cometh. [Cf. Matt. 25:4–6]
Glory be to the Father, and to the Son, and to the Holy Ghost.

128.

Emendemus in melius

Let us make amends for the sins we have committed in ignorance, lest we should suddenly, at the day of death, seek a place of repentance, and not be able to find one. Harken to us, God, and have pity on us, because we have sinned against thee.
Memento: Remember, man, that dust thou art and unto dust thou shalt return. [Cf. Gen. 3:19]

129.

Quando ritrova

When I find my shepherdess
In the meadow, with the sheep in the pasture,
I approach her and greet her.
Then she replies to me: May you be welcome.
Then I say to her: O gentle shepherdess,
No less cruel than beautiful,
You fight against my happiness.
Alas, do not be so harsh to me.
Then she answers: I am well disposed toward your suit,
But if you have no money, go your way.

130.

Voi ve n'andat' al cielo

Ye go heavenward, ye eyes blessed and holy,
With your bright light and my songs;
While I, cold and with nothing to console me,
Would fain rise in flight,
Remain saddened in sorrow and tears.
Would that love do that to ye,
Ye eyes serene,
For then would ye see that
Which a pitying heart should have;
And if ye cannot see your own [heart],
Then look at mine which ye hold imprisoned within you.

131.

Da le belle contrade

From the fair regions of the East,
Brightly and cheerfully rose the dawn;
And I in the arms of my divine idol
Was rejoicing in such bliss as no human mind can grasp:
When I heard, after a burning sigh:
"Hope of my heart, sweet desire,
Thou art going, alas!
Thou leavest me alone. Farewell!
What will become of me, saddened and sorrowful?
Ah, cruel love,
Uncertain and brief are thy joys,
And it even pleases thee
That the greatest happiness should end in tears."
Unable to say more she held me fast,
Repeating the embraces in so many coils
That never ivy or acanthus made more.

132.

Qui au conseil

[This is a rhymed paraphrase of Ps. 1:1–2.]

Blessed is the man that walketh not in the counsel of the ungodly, nor standeth in the way of sinners, nor sitteth in the seat of the scornful.
But his delight is in the law of the Lord; and in his law doth he meditate day and night.

138.

D'une coline

As I walk upon a hill
In the gayest and greenest of seasons,
When everything smiles in the fields,
I see a red rose
Which surpasses every other flower in beauty.

I see it from afar,
And I love it dearly;
I wish to pick it,
And I stretch my hand toward it,
But, alas, it is in vain.

139. *Salve Regina*

Hail, Queen, mother of pity!
Our life, sweetness, and hope, hail!
To thee we cry, the exiled sons of Eve.
To thee we sigh, lamenting and weeping in this valley of tears.
Well then, our advocate, turn thy pitiful eyes upon us.
And show us, after this exile, Jesus, the blessed fruit of thy womb.
O merciful, O pious, O sweet Virgin Mary.

140. *Agnus Dei*

O Lamb of God, who takest away the sins of the world: have mercy
upon us.

141. *Sicut cervus*

As the hart panteth after the water brooks, so panteth my soul
after thee, O God.
My soul thirsteth for God, for the living God: when shall I
come and appear before God?
My tears have been my meat day and night, while they continu-
ally say unto me, where is thy God?   Ps. 42:1–3.

142. *Alla riva del Tebro*

On the bank of the Tiber, a youth I see,
A charming shepherd, a charming youthful shepherd,
Voicing his feeling there:
Be satisfied, O cruel Goddess, with my woe and pain.
But a dead man cannot say that sorrow kills him.
Alas, wretched fate!

143. *Requiem aeternam*

Rest eternal, Lord, give to them, and let light perpetual lighten
them. Thou, God, art praised in Sion; to thee is the vow performed in Jerusalem. Hear, O God, my supplication. All flesh
cometh unto thee.

144. *Penitential Psalm*

O Lord, rebuke me not in thy wrath: neither chasten me in thy
hot displeasure.
My heart panteth, my strength faileth me: as for the light of my
eyes, it also is gone from me.
They also that render evil for good are mine adversaries; because
I follow the thing that good is.   Ps. 38:1, 10, 20.

145. *Bon jour, mon cœur*

Good day my heart,
Good day my sweet life,
Good day my eye,
Good day my sweet heart,
Ah! good day, my pretty one, my sweet one,
Good day, my delight, my love,
My sweet spring time, my sweet new flower,
My sweet pleasure, my sweet dove,
My lark, my fair turtle-dove,
Good day, my sweet rebel.

146a. *Cara la vita*

My dear life, it is indeed true that no other flame I love, that no
other flame burns in my heart in a time so turbulent and wild.

146b. *Sanctus*

Holy, holy, holy, Lord God of hosts: heaven and earth are full
of thy glory. Hosanna in the highest.   [Cf. Isaiah 6:3]

147. *Allon, gay, gay*

Come now, gay, gay shepherds,
Come now, gay, gay, be joyous.
Follow me.
Let us go to see the King
Who was born to us from heaven.
Come now . . .
I shall make him a nice present,
What shall it be?
This flute which I have, so gay.
Come now . . .
I shall give him a cake
And I shall offer him a full bumper.
Come now . . .
Ho, ho, I see him,
He suckles well without his thumb.
Come now . . .

148. *Exurge, Domine*

Arise and help us, and deliver us, for thy name's sake.
Ps. 44:26.

149. *O vos omnes*

All ye that pass by, behold and see if there be any sorrow like
unto my sorrow.   Lamentations 1:12.

150. *Non vos relinquam*

I will not leave you comfortless; I will come to you and your
heart shall rejoice.   John 14:18; 16:22.

152. *Hic est beatissimus*

This is the most blessed evangelist and apostle John who, by
favor of outstanding love, deserves to be honored by God above
all others.

155. *Madonna mia gentil*

My gentle lady, I thank love
Who has taken my heart
Giving it to you,
Who are not only beautiful
But adorned with such virtues that
While being on earth I seem to enjoy Paradise.

156. *Ecce quomodo*

I. Behold the righteous man perisheth and no one layeth it to
heart. Just men are taken away and no one considereth it. The
righteous man is taken away from the face of iniquity, and his
memory will be in peace.
II. His place is made in peace and his habitation in Sion. And his
memory will be in peace.

157. *In ecclesiis*

Praise the Lord in the congregation, Alleluia,
In every place of worship praise him, Alleluia.
In God, who is my salvation and glory, is my help, and my hope is
in God, Alleluia.
My God, we invoke thee, we worship thee; deliver us, quicken us,
Alleluia.
God our advocate in eternity, Alleluia.

158. *L'Acceso*

More than any other, Chloris,
You are beautiful and charming,
And your countenance delights every soul.

Indeed I burn for you inwardly
And outwardly, my fair sun,

And you are cruel toward my tortures,
You refuse even a single look as a reward.

160. *Al suon*

At the sound [of the music] the heart rests not,
But it increases the cruel ardor;
For yours are not songs,
But poisonous charms.   (6 stanzas)

161. *Io pur respiro*

In such anguish I still breathe,
And you still live, oh pitiless heart!
Ah, that there is no longer hope
Of seeing once again our well-beloved!
Oh death, give us help:
Kill this life;
Merciful, wound us, and let a single blow
To life give an end and to great woe.

164. *Quia vidisti me*

Thomas, because thou hast seen me thou hast believed: blessed
are they that have not seen and yet have believed.
John 20:29

165. *Ach Schatz*

My love, I complain to you about my great grief
Which I must bear.
O sweet solace of my life, turn to me,
Be friendly with me,
Convert my woe into joy,
Else I shall soon perish in despair.

166. *Factus est*

There came a sound from heaven as of a rushing mighty wind.
Acts 2:2.

167a. *Vater unser im Himmelreich*

Our father in heaven, who desirest all of us to be like brothers,
and to adore thee, to pray to thee: grant that not the mouth only
may pray, but that [the prayer] may come from the depths of
the heart.

168. *So wünsch ich ihr*

(1) Thus I wish her good night
    At a hundred thousand hours.
(2) If I consider her love,
    All my grief disappears.
(3) When I see her she delights me;
    She has captured my heart,
    Therefore my heart burns and I cannot forget her.
                                        (3 stanzas)

INDEX

Reference is made to item numbers, not pages. Ordinary figures (roman type) refer to the items themselves together with the related article in the Commentary; italic figures refer to the Commentary alone. Titles of compositions are italicized, names of composers in capitals and small capitals.